Reader's Digest BASIC GUIDE
Home Decorating

Contents

THE TEXT AND ILLUSTRATIONS IN THIS BOOK ARE TAKEN FROM THE READER'S DIGEST
'COMPLETE DO-IT-YOURSELF MANUAL' PUBLISHED BY THE READER'S DIGEST ASSOCIATION LIMITED
LONDON   NEW YORK   CAPE TOWN   MONTREAL   SYDNEY

Decorator's dictionary

Bleeding A fault which occurs when soluble paints or other materials on a surface dissolve and show through subsequent coats of paint.

Brushing out Spreading paint to form an even film over the surface.

Butt-joining Joining strips of wallpaper or other wall-coverings edge-to-edge, so that there is no overlap.

Cross-lining Hanging lining paper horizontally so that joins will not coincide with the vertical ones of the final layer of paper.

Cutting in Painting up to an edge; use a brush with an angled end for fine work.

Filler An inert material for filling holes and cracks—usually cellulose filler.

Grout A waterproof, cement-based paste, used to fill the gaps between ceramic tiles.

Knotting A solution of shellac and methylated spirit for sealing knots so that resin will not bleed through the paint.

Laying off The final brush strokes that leave a surface perfectly smooth. Lay off in the direction of the grain on wood and in the longest direction on metal.

Primer The first coat of paint on new work. It seals the surface and prevents oil in subsequent coats of paint from soaking into it; not to be confused with undercoat.

Selvedge The waste strip down both sides of a piece of wallpaper to protect the edges of the pattern from damage in storage and transit. It must be trimmed off before the paper is hung. Some papers are now sold ready trimmed and packed.

Size A solution of glue used to seal a surface before hanging wallpaper. It prevents water in the paste from being absorbed by the surface so that the paste is allowed to set.

Stopping A plastic material for filling holes and cracks in timber before painting. Examples are putty and white lead hard-stopping for exterior work around windows and doors.

Undercoat Used mainly to provide a good key for a gloss finish; it also makes an additional protective covering and an effacement when a colour is changed.

Metrication

Some building and decorating materials are now sold in metric measurements only, some in both metric and imperial measures, while others are still retailed in imperial measurements only.

In case a retailer is still working with only imperial measurements, it is advisable to know your requirements in both metric and imperial measurements. Conversion tables appear on p. 47.

In this manual, the available metric size, or a conversion, is followed by the imperial size in brackets. However, where a measurement is repeated on the same page, the imperial size is given once only.

Measurements which are not critical have been rounded up or down from their straight conversions of imperial measurements.

Tools for the job

WITH THE right equipment, decorating takes less time and effort and good results are more easily attained. The items shown here are for paperhanging and painting; the step-ladder can be used with the hop-up and scaffold board to make a working platform.

Try to take the long view when choosing decorating equipment. Often, only a few pence separate shoddy tools from others that will give years of efficient service.

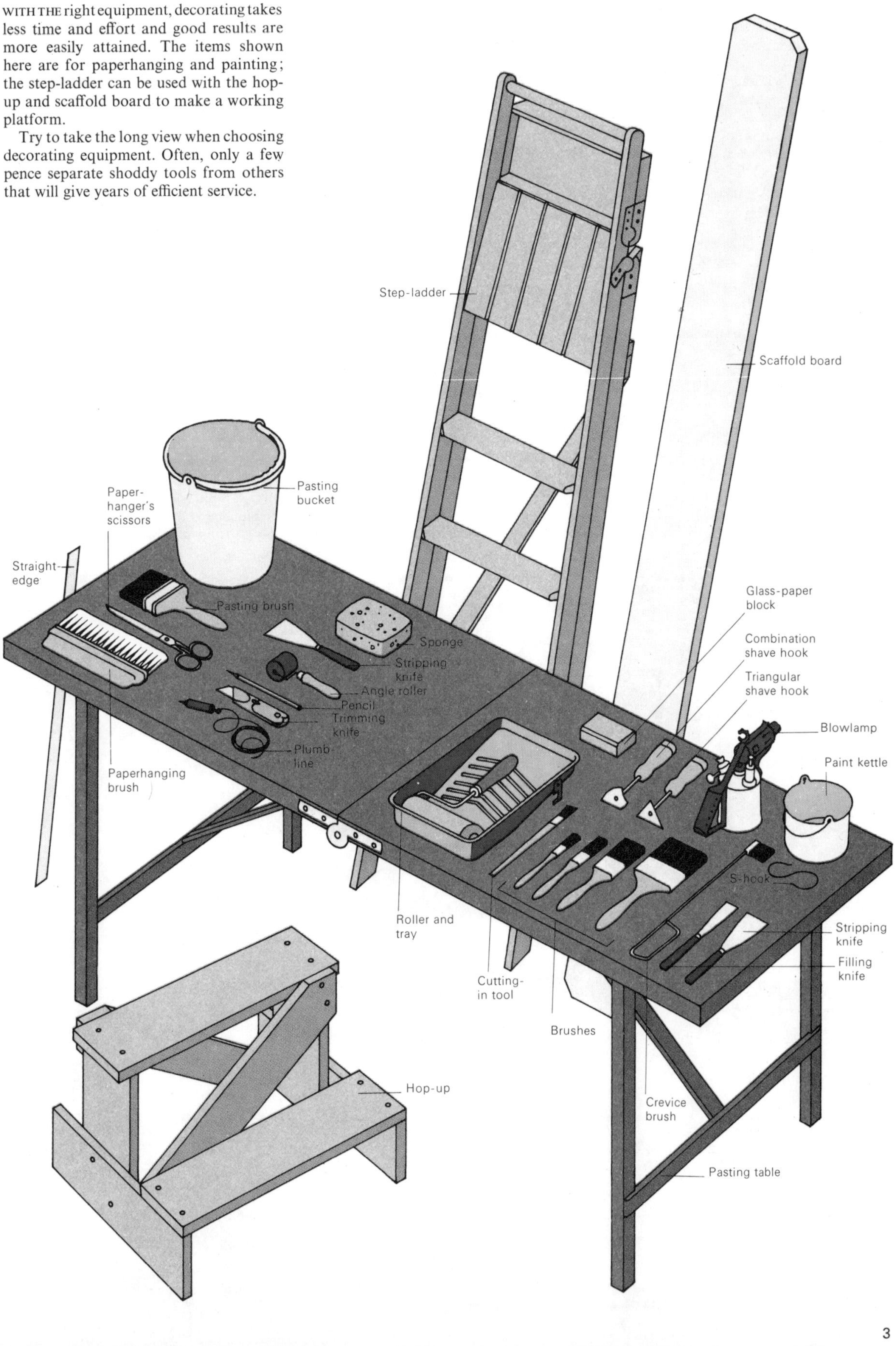

Step-ladder

Scaffold board

Paper-hanger's scissors

Pasting bucket

Straight-edge

Pasting brush

Glass-paper block

Sponge

Combination shave hook

Stripping knife

Triangular shave hook

Angle roller

Pencil

Blowlamp

Trimming knife

Paint kettle

Plumb line

Paperhanging brush

S-hook

Roller and tray

Stripping knife

Filling knife

Cutting-in tool

Brushes

Hop-up

Crevice brush

Pasting table

3

Brushes and rollers

For good results in painting you need a good brush, and the quality of a brush depends on its bristles.

Natural bristle, from the pig or boar, is the best. The natural taper gives the brush its shape; the rough surface of the bristles holds the paint; and the split ends, or 'flags', help you to apply the paint in a smooth, even coat. The synthetic material nearest to bristle is nylon.

Your choice of brush will probably depend on how much you are prepared to pay. It might be as well to buy a cheaper brush for priming and a better quality one for top coats. But since all new brushes shed hairs, use them for undercoating before using them for a final coat.

General-purpose brushes

You can do most indoor painting jobs, apart from ceilings and walls, with three sizes of brush: 50, 25 and 12 mm. (2, 1 and ½ in.) widths.

If possible, keep one set of brushes for white paint only and another for colours. No matter how well brushes are cleaned there is a chance that a brush once used for colour may contain old pigment which will bleed into white paint.

The brush sizes for ceilings and walls are 100 and 150 mm. (4 and 6 in.). Good quality brushes in these sizes are expensive, but they will last a lifetime if well looked after. Most amateurs will find the 100 mm. brush useful and quite adequate for large surfaces. The 150 mm. brush is rather unwieldy in unpractised hands.

Special brushes

The cutting-in tool is a useful brush for the difficult job of painting window-frames. With a little practice, the angled tip can be used to paint very straight lines.

If you do not wish to buy a cutting-in tool, a well-worn 12 mm. brush can do almost as good a job.

The crevice or radiator brush is a versatile brush for getting into tight corners; the wire handle can be bent to any angle.

The small crevice brush (below) is best for painting behind pipes. The round head enables you to apply paint in any direction.

The dusting brush is simply a soft brush used to clean the surface to be painted.

Rollers

Rollers do a much quicker job than brushes, and often give a superior finish, but they tend to use more paint.

If you use a roller, brushwork can be confined to tight corners where rollers cannot reach, or to unusually rough surfaces where rollers cover only the high spots.

Rollers can be used with almost any type of paint. They are less tiring to work with than a brush, especially on large areas.

You can buy rollers covered with a variety of materials. Mohair and foam rollers are best for gloss paints and distemper. Foam rollers leave a coarser stipple than lambswool or mohair and also splash easily. Replacement sleeves can be bought to replace worn roller surfaces.

After use, rollers and tray should be cleaned with paint solvent or, if emulsion paint was used, washed in warm soapy water. Allow them to dry before wrapping in paper for storage.

Wrap the tray in heavy paper after greasing it slightly to prevent rust. Clean it thoroughly before you use it again.

Pads

Mohair paint pads are more economical in use than rollers and are particularly suitable for covering uneven surfaces such as embossed paper. They can be used with emulsion and oil-bound paints, but it is recommended that the largest pad be used only to apply emulsion.

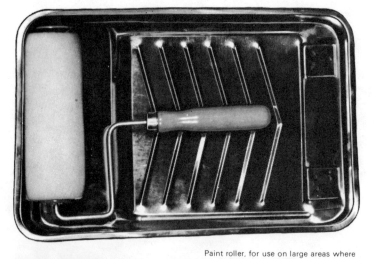

Paint roller, for use on large areas where it will do a quicker job than a brush and will often produce a better finish

For walls and ceilings, use a 100 or 150 mm. (4 or 6 in.) brush. Though expensive, these brushes will last a lifetime with proper care. Most amateur handymen will probably find the 100 mm. the easier to handle

Cutting-in tool, used on window-frames and for painting straight lines

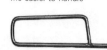

Crevice brush, useful for painting awkward corners, especially behind pipes

Paint pads can be used indoors and outdoors. The different sizes up to the 63 mm. (2½ in.) pad can be bought separately or in packs

These 50, 25 and 12 mm. (2, 1 and ½ in.) general purpose brushes are suitable for most indoor painting apart from walls and ceilings

Cleaning

Any brush, regardless of what it costs, will last longer if you look after it.

To clean most of the paint out of a freshly used brush, lay it on at least three thicknesses of newspaper and gently run the back of an old kitchen knife, or smooth scraper, from the heel of the bristles to their tips, squeezing out the paint.

Repeat this on the other side, and on the edges of narrow brushes.

Remove any paint from the metal binding and handle with solvent, and continue to clean thoroughly.

To clean off emulsion paint, simply use cold water.

For cleaning off oil-based paints, wash the brush in white spirit, and follow this by washing it in warm water, with soap or detergent. Finally, rinse away the soap.

Pay special attention to the heel—the area at the base of the bristles—as the paint tends to clog up there.

Do not force the brush out of shape by being too rough with the cleaning action.

Finding a brush coated with dried paint is a situation that faces most handymen from time to time. The only way of cleaning a hard brush is to soak it in a proprietary brush cleaner or in paint stripper. Take care not to get any of the stripper on the handle or it will strip off the varnish.

If the hardness has not set in, you might get results by soaking the brush in white spirit, but this will not work with emulsion paint, which is soluble only in water.

After soaking, remove the loosened paint with an old putty knife and re-immerse in the stripper or white spirit if more paint has to be removed. Finally, wash the brush in warm water.

Brushes which have hardened completely seldom come really clean at the base of the bristles.

There is nothing you can do about this: continued re-immersion will often lead to damaging the bristle bonding—and it is better to have a slight lump of old dry paint than no bristles.

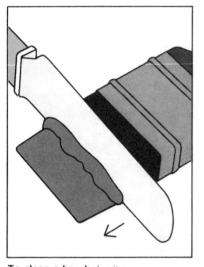

To clean a brush, lay it on a newspaper and gently run the back of a knife or a scraper along the bristles from heel to tip.

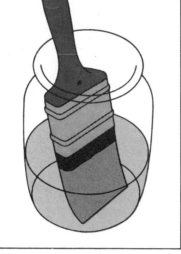

Wash the brush in water for cleaning off emulsion paint and in white spirit or brush cleaner for removing oil-based paints.

Remove final traces of oil-based paints with soap or detergent and warm water. Then give the brush a final rinsing.

Storing

Proper storing is as important as thorough cleaning if your brushes are to last.

When, after using a brush, you have cleaned it thoroughly and allowed it to dry, the best method of storing is to wrap it in newspaper. This helps to retain the shape of the bristles.

Unless the bristles are of nylon, keep a couple of mothballs in the drawer or cupboard where you store your brushes, to protect them from moths.

If you have finished painting for the day, but intend to carry on the following day, you can leave an oil paint brush in water overnight without going through the process of cleaning it.

Drill a hole in the handle, if one is not already there, and suspend the brush in the water—do not allow the bristles to touch the bottom of the container. The water level should just cover the heel of the bristles. Before you continue painting, shake the water out of the brush and wipe it dry on a rag or paper.

If you are using emulsion paint, it is a simple matter to run the brush under a cold tap. This must be done quickly—the brush will harden if you leave it.

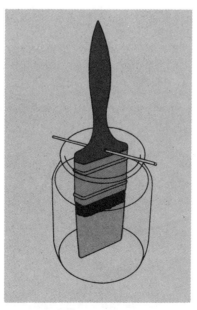

Overnight storing: suspend the brush in water, passing a nail or thin dowel through a hole bored in its handle.

Storing for longer periods: when the brush has been thoroughly cleaned and dried, wrap it in newspaper.

Painting equipment

Scrapers, knives and containers

Use a 75 mm. (3 in.) wide stripping knife for stripping paint off flat surfaces, and a triangular or combination shave hook for mouldings and difficult corners.

Most plaster cracks can be filled using a filling knife or a stripping knife. The blade on a filling knife is the more flexible of the two, and generally the filling knife is the more suitable.

For big jobs, such as painting walls or ceilings, it is convenient to pour the paint, as you need it, into a container. The best type is the polythene paint kettle, which is light and easy to clean.

The more traditional galvanised kettles are about the same price, but cleaning them is more difficult; burn out dried paint by setting light to it with meths.

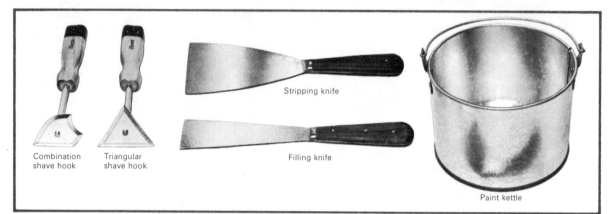

Combination shave hook

Triangular shave hook

Stripping knife

Filling knife

Paint kettle

Setting up a working platform

A step-ladder, preferably with a folding platform or a clip-on tray at the top, is essential for most painting.

For high work, above 2·5 m. (8 ft), use two step-ladders supporting a scaffold board. Below 2·5 m., a pair of hop-ups and a scaffold board provide the best platform.

With either of these arrangements you will be able to paint walls and ceilings without constantly getting up and down to move ladders along.

Scaffold boards, 250 × 32 mm. (9 × 1¼ in.) and up to 5·7 m. (18 ft) long, are obtainable from timber merchants or can be hired. Usually the most useful size of board is one about 3 m. (10 ft) long. Boards longer than this need support in the centre as well as at the ends.

A single hop-up is also handy. Being more portable than a step-ladder, it is ideal for painting just above head level.

Most decorating equipment can be hired if you do not wish to go to the expense of buying it.

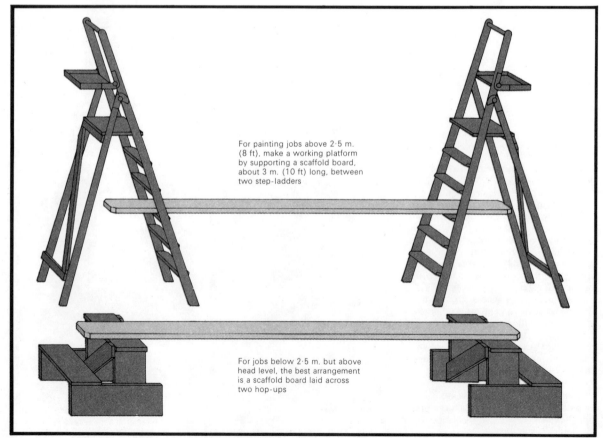

For painting jobs above 2·5 m. (8 ft), make a working platform by supporting a scaffold board, about 3 m. (10 ft) long, between two step-ladders

For jobs below 2·5 m. but above head level, the best arrangement is a scaffold board laid across two hop-ups

Types of paint

In the past, the range of paints available for household use was limited and it was difficult for the non-professional decorator to obtain first-class results with them. During recent years a number of new paints, designed for easier application and greater durability, have come on to the market.

Thixotropic or non-drip jelly paints give a smooth, glossy surface without the unsightly runs and sags an amateur might get with ordinary liquid paint. Most paints are available in jelly form.

It is generally better to repaint a gloss surface with gloss paint rather than with a water-thinned or emulsion paint.

Listed below are the paints most commonly used by the home decorator. The figures given for coverage apply to brush-work on an average wall or door surface, and are a guide only. The covering power of a paint varies according to the surface to be decorated, whether the paint is brushed on or applied by roller, and the skill of the decorator. One more point about coverage: one coat of jelly paint will often do the job of two coats of liquid paint, provided it is not brushed out.

Paint is now mostly sold in quantities of 500 ml., 1 litre, 2·5 litres and 5 litres. It is useful to remember that:

500 ml. is 12% less than 1 pint.　　　　　　2·5 litres is 10% more than ½ gallon.
1 litre is 12% less than ¼ gallon.　　　　　5 litres is 10% more than 1 gallon.

Type	Suitability	Finishes	Coverage	Notes
Oil-type paints Traditionally, these paints contained lead pigment, but the pigment is now usually based on titanium oxide and the paints are non-toxic. They are thinned with white spirit. Alkyd and other resins have largely replaced oil as a medium	Protecting timber and decorating window-frames, skirtings, architraves, doors, etc. Use gloss for outside work, all other finishes for indoor painting	Gloss, semi-gloss (also called lustre or eggshell) and matt	Liquid: 500 ml. covers approx. 9 sq. m. (90 sq. ft) Jelly: 500 ml. covers approx. 6·2 sq. m. (70 sq. ft)	All new surfaces must be primed first. Apply an undercoat for a liquid gloss paint. This is not necessary with jelly paints. Ask your dealer for details of paints with special qualities—heat resistance etc.
Emulsion paints Water-thinned, making it easy to clean brushes and remove splashes. Recent advances include co-polymer emulsions, which are claimed to have a higher resistance to moisture than ordinary paints	Interior walls and ceilings. Not suitable for use on woodwork, except as an undercoat. Exterior quality can be used indoors as well as outside	Matt or slight sheen	Liquid: 500 ml. covers approx. 7·5 sq. m. (80 sq. ft) Jelly: 500 ml. covers approx. 4·7 sq. m. (50 sq. ft)	First coats on very absorbent surfaces, e.g. bare walls, may be thinned with 1 part water to 4 of paint; otherwise thin with 1 part water to 8 of paint. Final coats are not normally thinned, but sometimes a little water allows easier brushing
Acrylic or semi-gloss emulsion Based on acrylic resins. They can be thinned with water	All interior surfaces	Semi-gloss and matt	Liquid: 500 ml. covers 6·5–7·5 sq. m. (70–80 sq. ft) Jelly: 500 ml. covers 4–4·8 sq. m. (40–50 sq. ft)	May be applied directly to a bare wall. Do not use it on metal surfaces without priming well first. Always fill and prime steel pins and screws—otherwise the steel will rust
Washable distemper Marginally cheaper than emulsion paint, but not as hard-wearing	Ceilings and interior walls	Matt	500 ml. covers approx. 9 sq. m. (90 sq. ft). Sold in 2 and 3 kg. tins containing approx. 1 and 1½ litres (¼ and ½ gal.)	Must be thinned before use: read the manufacturer's instructions. Stir well, and apply at least two coats. Wash lightly when dirty—do not scrub
Polyurethane (one-pack) Forms a hard surface which will stand up well to moisture and rough treatment	All interior surfaces, but do not use white on radiators—the heat discolours it	Gloss, semi-gloss and matt	500 ml. covers 6·2–9 sq. m. (65–90 sq. ft) depending on brand	With some brands, white tends to discolour. Check with your supplier

Stirring, storing and thinning

Thorough stirring is vital with liquid paints. Paint is made up of a suspension of fine particles in a liquid medium, and these particles tend to settle towards the bottom of the container.

If you have time, stand the can upside down for a day or so before use, to redistribute the particles.

Stir paint with a circular, lifting motion to ensure even distribution. Paint stirrers which fit on to an electric drill are available. Use them at a slow speed.

Jelly paints must not be stirred: they do not settle as other kinds do.

When paint is stored for any length of time after you have removed the can lid, a skin will form on the surface. Cut round this skin with a sharp knife, and try to lift it out in one piece.

Stir well and strain the paint through an old nylon stocking to remove any specks of skin that may have been left behind.

Small quantities of paint left over after a job are best stored in a screw-top jar. Label the jar with the name and colour of the paint and the room in which you used it—it will come in handy for touching up at a later date.

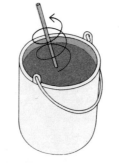

Stir paint with a lifting motion

Most paints can be thinned—emulsions with water, oil-based with white spirit. But do not thin jelly paints—it upsets the balance of the ingredients, and the paint loses its jelly and its covering power.

Check the instructions before using. When the paint is used, some of it usually runs down the side of the can and obscures the printing.

Strain paint through a nylon stocking, to remove odd specks of skin

Painting Indoors

New work

Wood. Sand the surface down so that it is quite smooth. Apply knotting to any knots and resinous patches, to prevent resin from 'bleeding' through the paint. Seal the surface with primer. Certain woods, including teak, cedar and resinous West African timber, require special primers.

Plaster, concrete and brick. In new houses, allow a 12-month drying-out period before you apply any gloss paint to these surfaces.

If you do not want to wait 12 months you can put on two coats of emulsion paint as a temporary measure. Emulsion paint allows the surface to breathe, and the wall can continue to dry out.

During the drying period, alkalis in the plaster and concrete cause a white surface deposit called efflorescence. This deposit should be wiped off, as it occurs, with a dry cloth.

Hardboard and wallboard. Make sure that the surface is perfectly clean and dry. Prime the surface and fill all pin and screw holes before painting.

Primer. Priming and undercoating are often thought to be the same, but in fact they are two separate processes. A primer is essential on new, unpainted surfaces, to prepare them for further painting. Undercoating helps to cover previous coats.

The type of primer you use depends on the surface you wish to paint. Detailed below are the most common building surfaces and the primers that are most suitable for them.

Some paint manufacturers, such as Bergers, have introduced 'all-surface' primers which, they claim, can be used for priming any surface—wood, metal, stone or plaster, hardboard, asbestos, etc.

Type of surface		Primer
Timbers	Ordinary softwood	Wood primer
	Ordinary hardwood	Aluminium wood primer
	Highly resinous wood	Aluminium wood primer
	Oily wood	Teak sealer or aluminium wood primer. Wash down with white spirit first
Building boards	Plasterboard	Plaster primer or thinned emulsion paint
	Hardboard	Hardboard primer or thinned emulsion paint
	Chipboard	Wood primer
	Asbestos and other fire-resistant boards	Alkali-resistant primer
Plaster, concrete, brick or stone		Alkali-resistant primer
Metals	Iron and steel	Red lead, calcium plumbate or zinc chromate primer
	Galvanised iron	Calcium plumbate primer
	Zinc sheeting	Calcium plumbate primer
	Aluminium	Zinc chromate primer (rub down first)
	Brass and copper	Zinc chromate primer (rub down first)
	Lead	No primer necessary

All set for painting

Before you start decorating a room, try to finish off all the odd jobs that need doing, such as replacing broken sash-cords, fixing badly fitting doors or having chimneys swept. If you leave these jobs until later, you will almost inevitably make a mess of your new paintwork.

Move the lighter pieces of furniture out of the room and stack the heavier pieces in the centre under dust sheets. Remove carpets and curtains and cover the floor, too, if it is tiled or of polished boards.

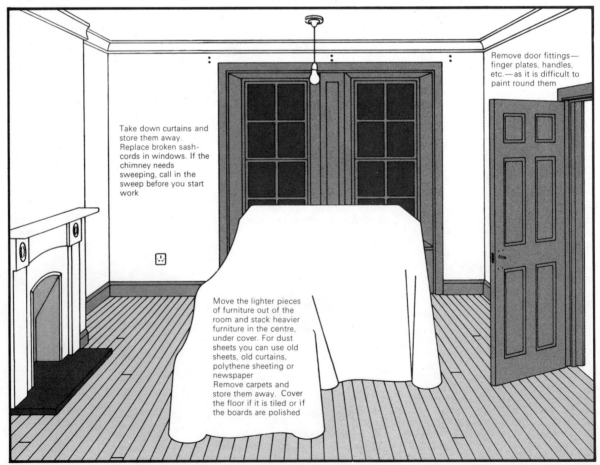

Remove door fittings—finger plates, handles, etc.—as it is difficult to paint round them

Take down curtains and store them away. Replace broken sash-cords in windows. If the chimney needs sweeping, call in the sweep before you start work

Move the lighter pieces of furniture out of the room and stack heavier furniture in the centre, under cover. For dust sheets you can use old sheets, old curtains, polythene sheeting or newspaper
Remove carpets and store them away. Cover the floor if it is tiled or if the boards are polished

Stripping paint

Strip paint only when there is no alternative. It is a tiring and time-consuming task. If the fault—blistering, flaking, etc.—is confined to small areas, you need to strip only the faulty section.

Do not strip paint just because a surface has been painted a number of times without being cleaned down. Very often the more coats of paint there are on a surface, the better protected it will be.

There are times when the paint must be stripped off in order to get a reasonable final surface. You can strip by scraping, burning off or using a chemical stripper. Each method involves hard work.

Scraping

Using a scraper, without the aid of heat or chemical, is very difficult, and is a technique that should only be employed on small areas.

A good scraper to use is the Skarsten type which has two blades—one serrated and the other plain. Use the serrated blade to score the surface, being careful not to go too deep; then use the plain blade to remove the rest of the paint. Use a shave hook for scraping mouldings.

Burning off

Burning is the quickest method of stripping paint. The best way to apply the heat is with a paraffin or gas blowlamp, although electric paint strippers are available.

Play the flame backwards and forwards across the surface. The idea is to melt the paint but leave the surface underneath untouched.

As the paint shrivels up, scrape it off, being careful not to let it fall on to your hand.

Keep a container on the ground to catch the melted paint.

Work from right to left if you are right-handed, and the other way round if you are left-handed.

For stripping mouldings, start at the top and work downwards, using a shave hook. On flat surfaces, work from bottom to top. When working on a moulded door, strip the mouldings first.

Make a habit of turning the blowlamp flame away from the surface while you are scraping; this way you will not burn any holes by accident.

Do not use a blowlamp on asbestos

Using a scraper: first, score the surface with the serrated blade.

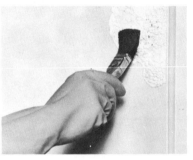

Stripping with chemicals: apply carefully—avoid making splashes.

sheeting, plaster walls or close to the glass in window panes.

Any charred patches on woodwork must be rubbed down, as paint will not adhere to them.

Electric strippers are much slower than blowlamps and they must not be used on damp surfaces.

Always remove curtains from windows before stripping paint—whether you are working indoors or outside.

Take care when stripping fascia boards to move any birds' nests or roofing felt out of the way—otherwise they can suddenly catch fire.

Do not use a blowlamp near thatched or wood shingled roofs.

After using a blowlamp, rub the surface thoroughly with medium glass-paper, knot, prime and apply stopping.

Chemical strippers

This method of stripping has one great advantage—you can scrape off paint right

Use the plain blade to remove the rest of the paint down to the bare wood.

Scrape off the blistered paint, wearing rubber gloves to protect hands.

up to a glass pane without cracking it.

Chemical strippers vary in their suitability for different jobs. Ask the advice of your retailer, and follow the instructions on the tin carefully.

This is particularly important if you are applying chemical strippers to metal, as some types may attack the surface.

Most of these strippers burn skin badly, so wear rubber gloves. Wear old clothes, too, and move anything which might get splashed.

When the chemical has done its work, strip off the paint with scraper and shave hook. Wrap stripped paint in newspaper and burn it immediately.

Do not leave the stripper can open or in a place where children might get at it.

After stripping, thoroughly clean the surface with white spirit and rub down with sandpaper. All traces of stripper must be removed, as any which remains will react against new paint. Knot, prime and apply stopping before repainting.

Burning off: strip mouldings first, working from the top of the door to the bottom.

Strip melted paint off mouldings with a shave hook or multi-edge scraper.

Use a scraper on flat surfaces. Strip each panel separately, starting from the bottom.

Preparing existing paintwork

The quality of paintwork, no matter how well the final finish is applied, depends upon the care taken in preparation. For instructions on repairing damage, such as cracks, bubbles, crazing, etc., see the facing page.

To sand down a wall, use abrasive paper wrapped round a sanding block.

For the best finish on woodwork, use 400 grade wet-or-dry paper, in the wet state.

Gloss and semi-gloss
Sponge the surface down with warm water and detergent. Rinse with clean water to remove all traces of detergent.

Rub down walls with abrasive paper to provide a key for the new paint, holding the paper over a cork sanding block, or any block of wood that fits comfortably into your hand.

A soda block is very coarse and is best kept for rubbing down paintwork containing sags, runs or other large blemishes.

For final rubbing down of woodwork, or after rubbing with a soda block, use fine sandpaper or wet-or-dry paper, 280–400 grade.

Grade 400 wet-or-dry is the finest grade, and when used wet it gives a good key for subsequent coats.

Rub down small damaged areas thoroughly to remove all unsound material. Fill first and sandpaper afterwards, so that there is no 'step' between the damaged area and the sound paintwork.

Knot and prime any areas of bare wood.

Emulsion paint, washable distemper
Sponge down thoroughly with water and detergent, and rinse.

Scrape off any loose or flaking paint and sand down to provide a smooth surface. Prime any bare patches.

Non-washable distemper
Always remove non-washable distemper before redecorating. It is made from whiting and soluble glue, and is easily washed off. This distemper is used mainly on ceiling paper.

Soak the surface with water two or three times, then scrape the paint and paper off with a broad stripping knife, holding a dust-pan underneath to catch the paint.

Be careful not to dig the stripping knife into the plaster.

Wash the surface down thoroughly afterwards to remove all traces of glue, whiting and old paper.

Wallpaper
If the paper is stuck firmly to the wall, there may be no need to remove it.

The two main dangers in painting over paper are that the inks in the pattern may 'bleed' through the paint film, and that the solvents in the paint may dissolve the glue holding the paper to the wall.

If you are satisfied that the paper is firmly stuck to the wall, simply dust it down with a soft brush and repair any tears or breaks by re-sticking them.

To test for bleeding, dab some of the paint you are going to use over a small area of the paper. If the ink does show signs of bleeding, either seal the paper with a

Use a power drill and wire brush for rapid removal of paint and rust from metalwork.

primer or strip it off altogether. Soak it before stripping.

Emulsion over wallpaper
After you have applied the last coat of emulsion, the paper may bubble.

These bubbles may disappear on drying, but if not, one of two courses is open:
1. Cut out the bubbles and re-stick.
2. If the bubbling is very bad, strip the wall and start again. (For stripping wallpaper, see p. 22.)

Paint over washable papers
Washable wallpaper should be sponged down with a mild detergent solution before it is painted. Rinse down after sponging.

Make sure that the paper is adhering to the wall properly and test the ink to see if it is going to bleed through the paint. Prime any worn patches.

Varnish and wood stain
Rub down thoroughly with sandpaper, to remove as much of the finish as possible.

Prime any bare wood. Seal wood stain with two coats of aluminium wood primer before painting. For a quick job, rub down to remove the shine, then prime and paint; this may well result in a finish that chips easily, so it is not suitable for skirtings.

Adhesion between paint and an old varnished surface is not good, even after rubbing down. To obtain a satisfactory surface which will not chip, it is best to chip off the varnish and treat the woodwork as for new work.

Silicone polish
Many polishes these days contain silicone, and this must be removed completely

An orbital sander is useful for smoothing down large areas of flat paintwork.

before you paint. If any traces are left on, the paint will flow away from those parts of the surface.

Rub the surface with coarse hessian or rough cloth dipped in white spirit, turning the cloth frequently to avoid spreading the polish. Finally, clean off with sandpaper.

Sometimes these polishes are very difficult to remove, so make a test on a small, unimportant area. If the paint separates as it is applied, the surface is not clean.

French polish
Rub over with methylated spirit, then sand lightly to remove final traces of polish.

Wax polish
Remove with white spirit and rub down with sandpaper.

Iron and steel
An electric drill with wire brush attachment is a very useful tool for preparing these surfaces.

Rub the surface down hard with a wire brush and emery cloth to remove all rust and loose, flaking paint.

Clean down with white spirit and prime any bare patches of metal. Rub down sound paint to a smooth surface.

Aluminium
Rub the surface down with fine abrasive paper and clean off with white spirit. Prime any bare patches before painting.

Other metals
Remove any loose surface material with abrasive paper or a wire brush. Seal with primer before painting. For all metals, see the section on New work, p. 8.

Making good

Some of the faults that mar paintwork are avoidable if you think ahead when decorating. Prevention is easier than cure, but when these faults—or others which cannot be foreseen—do occur, they can usually be put right.

Blisters and bubbles
Usually caused by moisture or resin trapped in wood beneath the paint surface.

Cut out the blistered paint with a knife, and clean out under the blister. Then knot or prime, fill with stopping, and sand the area so that there is no 'step' between it and the surrounding surface.

Allow the sanded surface to dry out properly. Then prime all bare and filled areas before repainting.

Cracks
This is a common fault in plaster walls.

Fill hair-line cracks with Alabastine, wider cracks with cellulose filler, such as Polyfilla, and large ones with plaster.

Rake out all loose material from the crack and, if necessary, cut it back to provide a firm edge. Dust down with an old brush.

Mix the filler to a fairly stiff consistency, dampen the crack and press the filler home. Smooth the surface down with your filling knife.

When the filler is dry, sand it back to the level of the surrounding surface with medium glass-paper. Use Alabastine to bring up any small dents.

Fill wide cracks in two or three stages, allowing each layer time to dry. Plaster

and Polyfilla tend to dry slightly harder than the surrounding surface.

A good technique is to fill cracks nearly to the top with these materials and give a finish with Alabastine, which can be cleaned off to the level of the wall more easily.

Crazing
The result of applying one type of paint over another, entirely different, type. The original paint expands and contracts at a different rate from the new paint and so causes it to crack.

If the fault is extensive, the entire surface must be stripped down and repainted. You may be able to remedy small areas of crazing by rubbing down with wet-or-dry paper and putting on a new top coat.

Chips and dents
To repair deep chips, remove any loose paint, prime any bare patches and fill with stopping or Polyfilla.

Sand the filler down to the level of the surrounding surface when it is dry. Give the filler a sealing of primer before repainting.

Efflorescence
A white deposit on plaster, concrete, brick and stone caused by alkaline salts working through to the surface.

Strip the paint off the affected area and allow to dry; then cover the surface with an alkali-resistant primer and redecorate.

Efflorescence is usually found in new houses, but it can continue for years if moisture continues to permeate a wall.

If it lasts for more than 18 months after a house has been completed, investigate the cause of the dampness and rectify it before attempting to cure the efflorescence.

Flaking
Some of the more common causes are: inadequate surface preparation before painting, moisture behind the paint film, efflorescence and the use of poor distemper in steamy conditions.

If the damage is extensive the surface must be stripped and carefully prepared before it is repainted. Make sure you use the correct primer.

Small areas of flaking may be treated in the same way as blisters.

Mould
Usually found in kitchens and bathrooms where the above-average temperature and humidity favour its growth.

Mould usually takes the form of small red, brown or black patches on the surface of the paint. It often occurs around steel window-frames in the putty line; but do not mistake the effects of rusting nail or screw heads for mould.

Treat with a fungicidal wash to kill the growth, and repaint if necessary.

Large areas of mould on walls which show signs of the plaster breaking down indicate damp penetration through the wall itself.

If mould is being caused by condensation, improve ventilation by fitting an extractor fan.

Filling holes: cut out any loose plaster, dust down, and damp lightly.

Fill large holes in stages; allow each layer to dry before putting in the next.

Smooth the final layer down with the filling knife and sand flat when dry.

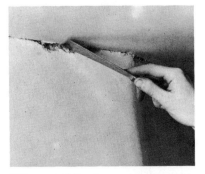

Filling cracks: rake out loose material. Cut back to a firm edge if necessary.

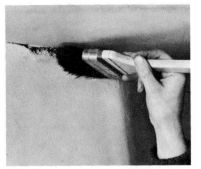

Dust down with an old brush to remove all loose material.

Press home the filler and leave it to dry; then you can sand it level.

Painting ceilings

If you are painting a complete room, work in this order: ceiling, woodwork, walls.

To get the right amount of paint on your brush, dip it into the paint until about one-third of the bristle length is covered, then press it against the side of the paint kettle or can. Do not drag the brush across the lip of the container, or you will remove too much paint. Jelly paints do not drip, so there is no need to remove excess paint from the brush.

All paint should be 'laid off' as you work—that is, smoothed over while the paint is still wet, and without dipping the brush or roller in fresh paint. Lay off woodwork in the direction of the grain.

To paint a ceiling you will need a pair of step-ladders or a couple of hop-ups, and a scaffold board.

Work in half-metre (2 ft) strips across the room, and always make your first strip the one nearest the window. Start by using the brush edge-on, to cut in where the ceiling meets the wall.

As you work along the strips, lay off the paint every metre (4 ft) or so.

500 mm. (2') strips

1 Start work by the window

Steps and scaffold board. Do not work from a single ladder—it is awkward and has to be repositioned continually

Use the brush edge-on, to cut in with a straight line where ceiling meets wall.

Turn the brush full-face, and continue painting in 500 mm. (2 ft) wide strips.

Lay off every metre or so, working from a wet edge back into the body of the paint.

Using a roller

Always use the specially designed sloping tray when painting with a roller. For best working the paint should come about one-third of the way up the slope.

Before starting work with the roller, paint in corners where it cannot reach, using a 25 mm. (1 in.) brush.

To load the roller, push it backwards and forwards in the paint, then run it up

to the top of the slope to remove any excess paint.

Cover the main part of the surface with alternating diagonal strokes of the roller, so that the strips of paint will be 'stitched' into one another, leaving no uncovered patches. Do not allow the roller to leave the surface suddenly, or it will splash.

When you come to laying off, work in

straight lines. Use vertical strokes for laying off walls, and lay off ceilings parallel with one of the walls.

Wash out the roller within a few minutes of completing the work.

Remember that rollers tend to use more paint than brushes, so allow for this when assessing how much paint you need to cover a wall or ceiling.

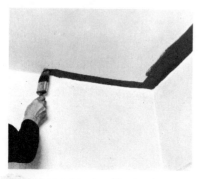 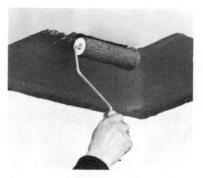 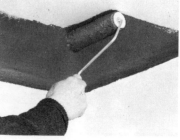

Begin by touching in with a brush corners a roller cannot reach.

Cover most of the surface with alternating diagonal strokes of the roller.

When you come to laying off, work with straight strokes of the roller.

Painting doors and windows

Flush and panelled doors

Panelled doors must be painted in a strict sequence. Do the whole job in one session: any pauses will result in the formation of a hard edge which is almost impossible to remove.

When painting the mouldings, make sure that your brush does not contain too much paint, because even a slight excess tends to accumulate and form 'tears'.

Paint the panels from each end, and work towards the middle.

When painting flush doors, start at the top and work down in sections. Work quickly, so that the paint does not harden before an adjoining section is painted.

Common faults
Bittiness. Small pimples on the surface of new paintwork, usually caused by dust.

Allow the paint to dry, then rub the surface down with fine 400 grade wet-or-dry paper. Apply a fresh finishing coat.
Curtain, sags and runs. These unsightly marks can be due to a number of causes. The paint may not have been spread in an even film, or too much paint may have been put on a surface.

Allow the paint to dry out properly, then smooth down the fault with fine wet-or-dry paper. Follow this with another finishing coat.
Grinning. When an old coat of paint shows through the new one.

Rub the surface down and apply an extra finishing coat—or more if they are needed.
Lifting. This happens when a new coat of paint pulls the old one away from the surface. It can be caused by applying the finishing coat before the undercoat is dry.

When the surface is thoroughly hardened, rub the affected area down with fine wet-or-dry paper and apply an undercoat before putting on another top coat.
Slow drying. Sometimes due to painting in cold weather, in which case the only answer is to wait; in time the paint will dry.

It may also be the result of painting over wax, grease or wet primer. If so, strip off the new paint, clean off, and repaint.
Uneven gloss. This fault usually indicates that the surface was not properly primed; prime the affected area and repaint.

It can also be caused by damp or frost affecting the paint while drying, in which case put on a second coat of gloss in more favourable weather.

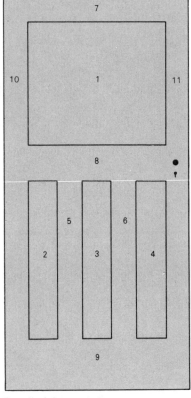

Panelled door painting sequence.

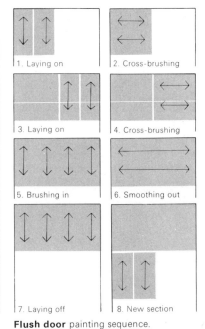

1. Laying on
2. Cross-brushing
3. Laying on
4. Cross-brushing
5. Brushing in
6. Smoothing out
7. Laying off
8. New section

Flush door painting sequence.

Casement and sash windows

As with doors, windows must be painted in strict order, governed by the way they are constructed. Paint casement windows in this order: [1] the rebates (where the glass joins the wood); [2] the cross-bars; [3] the cross-rails; [4] the hanging stile; [5] the meeting stile; [6] the window-frame.

An aluminium shield is available to keep paint off the glass when you are painting rebates. Do not use cardboard for this job.

To paint a sash window, first pull the bottom sash up and the top sash down, so that you can get at the meeting rail, then paint in this order: [1] meeting rail, including its bottom edge and rebate; [2] bars and stiles as far as you can go on the top sash; [3] bottom edge of the bottom sash; [4] the soffit; [5] 50 mm. (2 in.) down the inside of the outside runners.

Now almost close the window, and carry on by painting [6] the top couple of inches of the inside runners. Finish off in the same order as for a casement window.

When you paint the outside of the window, following the same method as for the inside, you will be able to paint [7] the bottom of the inside runners; and [8] a short way up the inside runners.

Thin the paint for all work inside run-

ners, to reduce the risk of sticking, and take care not to get paint on sash-cords, as it will weaken them. You do not need to paint the entire length of the runners—they are protected by the tight fit of the window sashes.

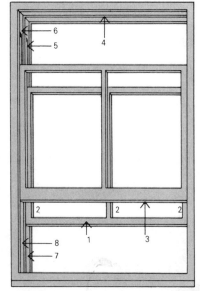

Casement window painting sequence.

Sash window painting sequence.

Painting walls

Different procedures for different paints

Plan your work so that you always complete an entire wall in one session. If you leave a half-finished wall overnight, or even break off for a meal, the line where you picked up the work will show through the finished surface.

Using gloss or semi-gloss paint

1. The wall will be covered in sections about 500 mm. (2 ft) square. Do not make them much bigger, or the paint will start to dry before you have a chance to brush it out. Start at the top right-hand corner (top left if you are left-handed) and cover the first square with vertical strokes.
2. Without reloading, brush over the section with horizontal strokes.
3. Still without reloading, brush over the surface again, both up-and-down and sideways, until the brush glides smoothly over the surface, indicating that the paint film is perfectly even. Reduce pressure as you brush out in this way, so that the brush marks will gradually be smoothed out.
4. Lay off the paint with vertical strokes.
5. Continue working in 500 × 500 mm. sections, until the surface is covered.

Take care not to apply a double coat at joins between sections. Work towards the join, allowing the brush to leave the surface gradually, so that the join will not show.
6. Do not brush undercoat and topcoat

in opposite directions, otherwise you will produce a 'cross-hatched' effect.

Using emulsion

1. Apply emulsion in bands of paint, about 200 mm. (8 in.) wide, across the wall. Start at the top and work down.
2. Brush out in the same way as for gloss

Using jelly paint

Thixotropic paints are designed to go on in one coat, and it is essential not to pull them out too far by overbrushing. Apply a full coat and brush it sparingly.

paint. Lay off upwards, in a criss-cross pattern.

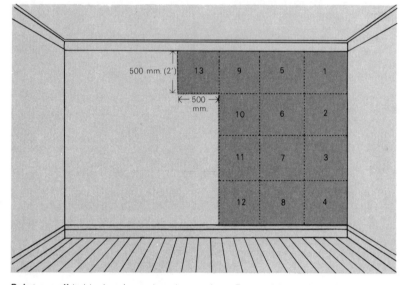

Paint a wall in blocks when using gloss, as here. For emulsion, paint in bands.

Gloss-painting a wall. Apply the paint with vertical strokes of the brush.

Without reloading, brush over each section with sideways strokes.

After you have brushed out, lay off from the wet edge back into the paint.

Using a spray gun

Spray painting is a lot more difficult than it looks. If you want to try it, the best idea is to get someone with experience to show you how. Listed below are a few important points to remember.
1. Use a spray gun only on a large area, such as a wall or ceiling. The effort involved in preparing a small job is out of proportion to the results. (An aerosol spray, though, is useful for small jobs.)
2. Mask off all areas you do not wish to paint, or you may ruin your decorating.
3. Thin the paint with the appropriate solvent thinner. Getting the right consistency is a matter of experience. Read the manufacturer's instructions carefully.
4. Never spray in an area that is not properly ventilated. Always wear a face mask.
5. Work with the gun at a point between 300 and 450 mm. (12 and 18 in.) away from

the surface, maintaining this distance all the time.
6. Keep the nozzle at right angles to the work. Do not swing the gun in an arc from side to side, because this will result in an uneven paint film.
7. Do not concentrate the spray on one area, or you will cause sags and runs.

8. Clean the gun after use.
9. The biggest problem facing amateur users of spray guns is lack of air pressure behind the gun.
10. Spray guns which attach to the exhaust end of cylinder vacuum cleaners seldom give a good spray. Rollers are more reliable and often quicker.

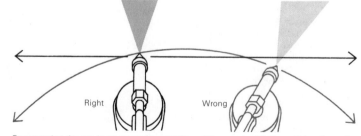

Do not swing the gun in an arc or the paint film will be uneven. Work parallel to the wall.

Treatment of surfaces

Damp, heat and frost while paint is drying are the enemies of the painter working outdoors. Damp will cause the paint to peel; a hot sun will cause blistering; and frost will cause gloss paint to become flat.

Work, therefore, in dry, warm weather after a dry spell. Do not start before the dew has cleared, and stop before it returns.

If you must paint during a wet spell, work on the dry side of the house and first wipe over the surface with a dry cloth.

When painting windows, check that putty is not loose or cracked. If it is, replace it.

Remember that preparation, though hard work, is the only way to get good results.

Always allow undercoats and first coats to dry properly before applying the final coat; and always rub down lightly between coats.

Wood

(a) New softwood
1. Smooth with a plane and glass-paper.
2. Apply knotting to knots and resinous patches, to prevent resin bleeding through.
3. Prime with a good quality primer.
4. Fill any holes or splits with water-resistant filler or stopping and, when it is hard, rub down with glass-paper. If holes are not sufficiently filled after rubbing down, repeat until the surface is level.
5. Dust off any particles, especially in crevices where the paint-brush can pick up dust, which will cause little lumps in the finished surface.
6. Apply an undercoat.
7. Apply at least one coat of gloss paint.

(b) Previously painted woodwork
(i) In poor condition (e.g. peeling and possibly bare in places):
1. Burn off the paint over the entire surface.
2. Remove any remaining paint with coarse glass-paper, using a scraper to clear out angles and corners.
3. Rub down with medium glass-paper to get a smooth surface.
4. Apply knotting to knots and resinous patches.
5. Prime the surface.
6. Fill any cracks or holes with filler or stopping, rub down the filled areas and touch them in with undercoat.
7. When the filled patches are dry, lightly rub down with medium glass-paper and apply an undercoat.
8. Apply a gloss coat—two if you want extra protection.
(ii) In reasonable condition:
Rub down with medium glass-paper, and continue as for stages 6, 7 and 8 in (b) (i) above.

(c) Hardwoods and cedar cladding
Preservatives and clear varnishes give a better finish than paint.
1. Use a Skarsten scraper to remove any old linseed oil or sealer on hardwoods; sandpaper cedar, or use Translac 'Colorbac', to remove grey powdering.
2. If any filling is necessary, use putty stained to match the timber.
3. Rub down with glass-paper and apply two coats of preservative.
4. Varnish if required.

Stone and brickwork, rendering

(a) Previously painted stone or brick
(i) If using cement paint:
1. Brush off loose particles and grime with a stiff brush.
2. Fill any cracks or holes with mortar.
3. Apply two coats of paint.
(ii) If using exterior grade emulsion:
1. Make good any holes or cracks, brush off any loose particles.
2. Seal with a thinned coat of emulsion.
3. Apply two coats of emulsion.
(iii) If using gloss paint:
1. Remove flaking paint with a scraper or wire brush.
2. Repoint where necessary.
3. Apply sealer to any bare patches.
4. Apply an undercoat (when covering a dark colour with a light one, apply two).
5. Apply a coat of gloss.

(b) New stone or brick
(i) Cement paint:
1. To prevent efflorescence—salts in the wall working through to the surface, where they appear as whitish deposits—apply a special sealer. The supplier will advise which one to use.
2. Apply two coats of paint.
(ii) Emulsion paint:
1. Fill any holes and joints.
2. Apply the correct sealer (with some makes, this can be made of emulsion thinned with water).
3. Apply two coats of exterior grade emulsion.
(iii) Gloss paint:
As for (a) above, but there will be no defective pointing to replace.

(c) Old rendering and pebble-dash
(i) Cement paint and emulsion:
As for (a) above, except that a soft brush, slightly dampened, should be used to brush down pebble-dash, and you may have to use a stippling brush to paint pebble-dash and stuccoed surfaces.
(ii) Gloss paint:
As for (a) above, except that there will be no repointing.

(d) New rendering and pebble-dash
(i) Cement paint and emulsion:
As for old rendering and pebble-dash.
(ii) Gloss paint:
Brush off. Apply a special sealer to prevent efflorescence, then carry on as for stages 4 and 5 in (a).

Metal

(a) New ferrous metal (steel, cast iron, etc.)
1. Wipe off any oil or grease with a rag dipped in turps substitute.
2. Remove any rust with a wire brush, then dust off.
3. Apply a coat of the correct metal primer (when buying metal primer, tell your paint merchant what kind of metal you are priming and where it is situated).
4. Lightly rub down and apply two coats of gloss paint.

(b) Old ferrous metal with extensive rust
Thoroughly scrape and wire brush the surface. An electric drill with a wire brush attachment will cut down time and effort. Continue as for stages 3 and 4 in (a) above.

(c) New galvanised metal
1. Wipe off any oil or grease with a rag soaked in turps substitute.
2. Apply a coat of calcium plumbate, or a similar special primer, which will provide a key for the paint.
3. Apply an undercoat.
4. Apply a gloss coat.

(d) Old galvanised metal
Chemical paint removers may damage the galvanising, so remove loose paint with a wire brush. Use the brush carefully as scratches in the metal will allow rust to form. Continue as for (c) above.

(e) New non-ferrous metal (aluminium or alloys)
1. Clean off oil or grease with a rag dipped in turps substitute.
2. Apply the appropriate primer.
3. Rub down very lightly and apply two gloss coats.

(f) Corroded non-ferrous metal
1. Lightly scrape off or wire brush away the corrosion, which shows as a white crystalline deposit. Do not scratch surface.
2. Apply zinc chromate or a similar primer.
3. Lightly rub down and apply two coats of gloss.

Other surfaces

(a) New asbestos
Emulsion:
As for stone and brickwork (b).
Gloss:
1. Fill any holes and joints and rub down.
2. Brush off and prime with an asbestos primer.
3. Apply an undercoat.
4. Apply a coat of gloss.

(b) Old asbestos
Emulsion:
As for stone and brickwork (a).
Gloss:
1. Rub down and scrape off any loose particles.
2. Fill holes and joints and touch up bare patches with undercoat.
3. Undercoat the entire surface.
4. Apply a coat of gloss.

(c) New hardboard
Gloss:
1. Fill nail holes and joints and rub down.
2. Brush off and apply a coat of hardboard primer or aluminium flake primer.
3. Apply an undercoat.
4. Apply a gloss coat.
Note: paint the back and edges of the hardboard to keep out damp.

(d) Old hardboard
Gloss:
1. Fill holes and joints, rub down, scrape off loose paint and brush off loose particles.
2. Touch in bare patches with undercoat, then continue as for stages 3 and 4 in (c) above.

Painting outdoors/2

Order of working

Complete all burning down and rubbing off before you start painting, so that dust and flakes will not fall on to wet paint.

When you move on to the painting stage, start with the surfaces for which you need a large brush (e.g. cement renderings). Almost inevitably, some paint will get on to surrounding surfaces, and 'cutting in' is best done with a small brush at the under-coating stage.

The order of working for painting the entire outside of a two-storey house is shown below.

1. Clean out the gutters, repair any defective joints on metal guttering, apply two coats of bitumastic paint to the inside and wire-brush the outside.
2. Clean off asbestos soffits with a stiff brush or medium glass-paper.
3. Rub down sound paint on the wood-work, to provide a key. Burn off loose or flaking paint and apply priming to any bare patches of wood.
4. Wire-brush the rest of the metalwork, treat any corroded spots with rust remover, and prime any bare patches.
5. Wire-brush the rendering, fill, seal and apply a coat of cement paint or exterior grade emulsion (two coats for extra protection).
6. Fill and undercoat the doors and wood surrounds to windows.
7. Give asbestos soffits two coats of emulsion or one of undercoat.
8. Working from the top, complete all undercoating, then gloss paint all under-coated surfaces. Give a second gloss coat for extra protection if necessary.

Points to note. When you repaint windows or doors, check that the extra thickness of paint will not result in the sash or door sticking. If this looks likely, plane off some of the edge to allow a clearance of a penny's thickness before painting.

Cut out all defective putty and replace it, with fresh linseed oil putty on wood sashes or with metal glazing putty on metal sashes.

Cleaning up. To clean paint spots off glass, wipe over with a leather, then scrape with a piece of Formica or similar material. Do not use a scraper or sandpaper as these will scratch the glass, though fine wire wool is both safe and effective.

With quarry tiles, scrape off the paint, wipe over with a turps-soaked rag, and wash with soap and water.

To clean up brickwork, scrape off paint marks, then use a wire brush. Work along the whole brick to prevent a patchy effect.

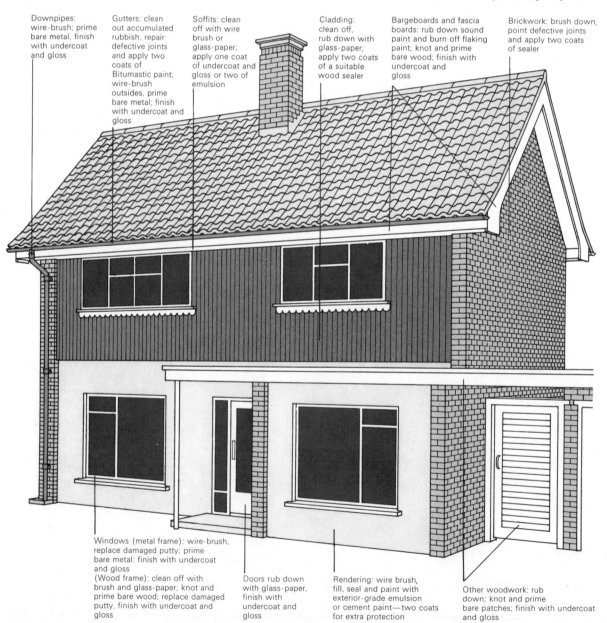

Downpipes: wire-brush; prime bare metal, finish with undercoat and gloss

Gutters: clean out accumulated rubbish, repair defective joints and apply two coats of Bitumastic paint; wire-brush outsides, prime bare metal; finish with undercoat and gloss

Soffits: clean off with wire brush or glass-paper; apply one coat of undercoat and gloss or two of emulsion

Cladding: clean off, rub down with glass-paper; apply two coats of a suitable wood sealer

Bargeboards and fascia boards: rub down sound paint and burn off flaking paint; knot and prime bare wood; finish with undercoat and gloss

Brickwork: brush down, point defective joints and apply two coats of sealer

Windows (metal frame): wire-brush, replace damaged putty; prime bare metal: finish with undercoat and gloss
(Wood frame): clean off with brush and glass-paper; knot and prime bare wood; replace damaged putty, finish with undercoat and gloss

Doors rub down with glass-paper, finish with undercoat and gloss

Rendering: wire brush, fill, seal and paint with exterior-grade emulsion or cement paint—two coats for extra protection

Other woodwork: rub down; knot and prime bare patches; finish with undercoat and gloss

Reaching the work

Ground floor windows can be reached from a hop-up, or from a board supported between step-ladders. To reach gutters, bargeboards and upper windows, you will need a ladder or scaffolding.

Ladders. The extension type of ladder is best because it can be adjusted to the height of the work. To erect a ladder by yourself, push its foot against the foot of the wall, lift the top end over your head, and walk towards the wall, raising the ladder rung by rung into the vertical position. Then pull the foot of the ladder out from the wall.

A helper can put a foot on the bottom rung and steady the ladder as you walk forward raising it from the ground.

The distance between the foot of the ladder and the wall should be about a quarter of the height of the ladder.

Extension ladders should be erected in the closed position, and extended when upright. Make sure that the locking device is well seated on its supporting rung.

If you are right-handed, start painting at the right-hand side of a window etc., so that as you move along the ladder will rest on surfaces that have not yet been painted.

Try to arrange the ladder so that as you work your shoulder will be level with the top. This gives plenty of ladder to hold on to, and makes sure that you will not be kept too far away from the work by the slope of the ladder.

Scaffolding. A scaffold tower costs more to hire than a ladder, and takes more time to erect and dismantle: once assembled it is more convenient to use than a ladder.

One easy-to-assemble tower, made by Scaffolding (Great Britain) Ltd., gives a safe working platform up to a height of about 9·8 m. (31 ft 8 in.) and can be hired.

If there is a firm, level surface around a building, sectional scaffold towers fitted with castor wheels, each with a locking device, can be helpful. You will be able to move the tower without dismantling it, but before you start working, make sure that you have locked the wheels.

Rigid safety standards are laid down for commercial firms using scaffolding, and it is worth copying them by using guard rails and toe boards.

A 5 m. (16 ft) mobile scaffold tower, including toe boards and decking boards, can be hired by the week, plus delivery and collection charges.

Types of ladder

The choice of ladders for household use is governed by two factors—the amount of covered storage space available and the maximum height that the ladder may have to reach. It is dangerous to overstretch when working at the top of a ladder: buy one which, when extended, is at least as tall as the highest point to be reached when using it.

Push-up extending ladders can be difficult for one person to manoeuvre into place. If the ladder has to be extended by more than 16 ft (5 m), obtain one that is rope-operated.

Builders' steps: it is useful to have two pairs of builders' steps and a scaffold board which can be fitted as a trestle between them

Extending ladders: these are either extended by hand or by pulley and rope

Platform steps: when work requires the use of both hands—for example, ceiling decoration—use steps with a platform on which to put paint or tools

Combination ladders: some types of household steps can be unfolded to make ladders. They are not suitable for very high work

Combination ladder-trestle: these have an extending section, as well as one which can be used with builders' steps and a scaffold board to form a trestle

Safety on the job

Ladders

Always examine a ladder for cracked or rotten rungs and for any loose joints.

Never rest a ladder against glass, glazing bars or plastic guttering.

Never overstretch to one side of a ladder: it may slide sideways.

Never stand on the top rungs of a ladder. The minimum safety position is about four rungs down.

Always leave at least a two-rung overlap between sections on a 14 ft (4·3 m) extension ladder; three rungs on a 16 ft (4·9 m) ladder.

Soft ground Stand the foot of the ladder on wide board, with a batten screwed across to prevent slipping

Wide overhangs Fix a stay, obtainable from builders' merchants, to position the ladder further out from the wall

Carrying Grip the ladder with one hand and support it above shoulder level with the other

Securing on a hard surface Place a bag of sand or soil against the foot of the ladder

Securing at top Tie ladder to a downpipe bracket or a ring bolt screwed to the soffit

Lifting Push the foot of the ladder against the wall. Work hands down the rungs to push it upright

Securing on soft ground Drive stakes into the ground and tie the sides of the ladder to them

Painting Hang the tin of paint on to a metal S hook. Always try to hold the ladder with one hand

Positioning Pull out the bottom. The ideal distance from the wall is about one quarter of ladder height

Uneven ground If the ground is uneven, cut and position wood blocks at the lower side of the ground

Climbing Always look straight ahead —not down or up. Be prepared for flexing on ladders that are very long

Scaffolding

The cheapest and simplest form of scaffolding that can be erected easily by one person is a sectional tower. The tower has castors on the bottom frame so that it can easily be moved along to new positions.

Its height should not exceed three times the minimum base dimension.

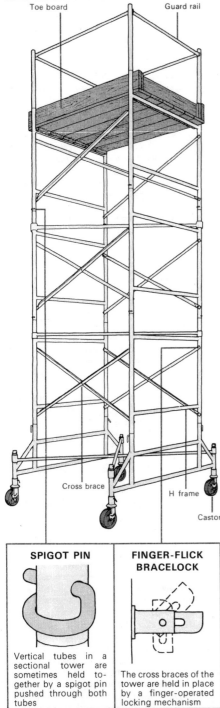

Toe board

Guard rail

Cross brace

H frame

Castor

SPIGOT PIN

Vertical tubes in a sectional tower are sometimes held together by a spigot pin pushed through both tubes

FINGER-FLICK BRACELOCK

The cross braces of the tower are held in place by a finger-operated locking mechanism

1 To erect a tower scaffold, first connect one frame and cross brace. Secure finger-flick bracelocks

2 Repeat on the opposite frame and cross brace. Join frames and fit horizontal cross brace to corners

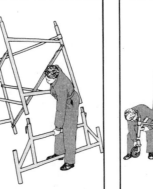

3 Position the completed unit on base frames provided and tighten the locking handles on the uprights

4 Fit two braces diagonally to the four corners of the tower base and lock in castor wheels or base plates

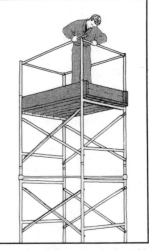

5 Lay temporary boards to stand on. Add further frames and cross braces, then lock in place with spigot pins

6 At the height required, add decking boards, guard rails, guard posts and toe boards

Paperhanging/1

Types of wallpaper

Machine-printed paper. This is the most common type of wallpaper. The design is printed on to the surface with rollers, in up to 20 colours.

The cheaper papers, known as 'pulps', have the design printed directly on to the paper, while the better quality and more expensive papers are coated with a 'ground' of colour before the design is printed.

Papers vary in weight, and the cheaper, thinner papers may stretch and distort if over-soaked with paste before you hang them. Thick papers can be useful to help conceal minor defects on a wall.

Hand-printed paper. This is produced by block, screen or stencil printing, and because of the amount of time taken in production it is expensive.

Hand-printed papers have the advantage that the designs are generally sharper because their production has been given a certain amount of individual attention, which machine-printed papers have not.

Embossed paper. This has the design pressed into it with a metal roller so that it stands out in relief. Imitation leather, textile and wood grain effects are produced by this process.

Duplex embossed papers have a deeper design than others and are produced by bonding two layers of paper together before the design is pressed out. This makes the paper more stretch-resistant.

Flock paper. This has the appearance of velvet. It is made by gluing silk, nylon or wool cuttings to the surface of the paper so that the design stands out in relief and has a noticeable pile.

Ingrain paper. An 'oatmeal' texture is given by the addition of small wood chips and sawdust to the paper pulp during manufacture.

The paper is usually emulsion painted after it has been hung, although pre-painted white ingrain paper is available.

Washable paper. A transparent coating of synthetic resin protects this paper from penetration by water, making it suitable for use in bathrooms and kitchens.

Most washable papers are very difficult to remove once they are up. The surface must be scored all over with a wire brush so that water can get through to the adhesive. Crown manufacture a washable paper called Cleen-Strip, which can be peeled off the wall without soaking, leaving behind it the smooth back paper which can be either left on as a lining or removed.

Washable papers are available with either a matt or glossy finish. Do not use detergent or abrasive materials to clean them—warm, soapy water is sufficient.

Ceiling paper. Papering ceilings is a more difficult job than wallpapering, but sometimes it is the only way to help disguise a badly cracked or uneven ceiling. An embossed paper is best for this job. Ceiling papers can be emulsion painted.

Lining paper. This is essential on some surfaces, such as painted walls, but it is advisable to use it before all wallpapering if first-class results are required. The lining paper gives the surface an even porosity, which helps when hanging the final layer of paper.

Lining papers are available in several weights. Use lighter papers on normal wall surfaces, heavier papers to help conceal an uneven surface. Always hang lining paper horizontally.

Pitch-coated lining papers are available for use on walls that are affected by dampness, and they should be pasted on the pitch-coated side.

Surfaces that are subject to movement, such as tongued and grooved woodwork and battened wallboards, can be lined with a cotton-backed lining paper. These papers should be pasted on the backed side.

Other wall coverings

Vinyl wall covering is made from a layer of cloth or paper-backed PVC, which can either be printed or given a textured finish.

This material is very tough and it will not tear when handled. It is also steam and water-resistant and can be scrubbed down with a soft brush when it gets dirty.

Because of vinyl's resistance to penetration, you must hang it with a special adhesive containing a fungicide—water behind paper could produce mould. A fungicide is already incorporated in the paste of ready-pasted vinyl.

Anaglypta is an embossed covering made from two layers of paper bonded together. There are more than 30 designs, and they can be given either a matt or silk finish with emulsion paint.

Superglypta is a deeply moulded cotton-based paper that is particularly strong. It looks like plaster, is good for covering badly cracked walls and ceilings and can be covered with emulsion paint.

Rolls of Anaglypta and Superglypta are 10·05 m. × 521 mm. (11 yds × 20½ in.).

Fabrics, such as dyed hessian or felt, are available in rolls prepared for hanging. The material can be backed with foam, paper or latex, making it much easier to handle. Unprepared furnishing hessian can also be hung on walls (see p. 28).

Japanese grasscloth is made from closely spaced strands of dried grass, sewn together and glued to a background paper.

Cork wall covering, made by gluing irregularly shaped cork panels to a background paper, gives an interesting textured effect.

Silk wall covering is made by gluing finely woven silk cloth to a background paper.

Mica prints. These papers have an attractive sheen, which may be achieved by adding mica either to the grounding to give the paper a satin-like surface, or to the inks to heighten the effect of the pattern.

Moirés. A watered silk effect, similar to moiré material and achieved by means of a fine emboss. This effect may also be reproduced on cheaper papers by printing.

Lincrusta is a putty-like material, made from linseed oil and fillers bonded to a flat backing paper. It is available in simulated wood panelling, or with textured effects.

Lincrusta is sold in rolls 10·06 m. (12 yds) long. Most widths are 533 mm. (21 in.); others vary between 457 mm. (18 in.) and 533 mm.

Most of the more expensive wall coverings are difficult to hang: it is better not to use them until you have mastered the techniques of wallpaper hanging.

Estimating and buying

Estimating. Most wallpaper is sold fully trimmed in rolls 10·5 m. (11 yds) long and 530 mm. (21 in.) wide. Some papers are still sold with a margin on either side called the selvedge. This must be trimmed off before the paper is hung, reducing the effective width of the paper to between 510 and 520 mm. (20 and 20½ in.).

To calculate the number of rolls needed for a job, first measure the height of the room. Then, bearing in mind the wastage due to pattern matching, work out how many lengths can be cut from one roll.

For example, if the room is 2·5 m. high, you get four lengths from a 10·5 m. roll.

Multiply the number of lengths by the trimmed width of the paper. In the example 4 lengths × (say) 500 mm. = 2 m.

Then divide this figure into the perimeter of the room to find the number of rolls needed. Bear in mind that you cannot usually buy fractions of a roll, so any remainder in the division sum will have to be made up to the next whole roll.

If the room in the example has a perimeter of 18 m., then 18 m. ÷ 2 m. = 9 rolls needed. If this method seems rather complicated, you can use a simple formula:

$$R = \frac{H \times P}{5}.$$ R is the number of rolls required, H the height of the room and P its perimeter, both in metres.

Ignore doors and windows if they do not cover a large area, and allow an extra roll for waste if using large-pattern paper.

Buying. If the paper has a selvedge, have it trimmed off in the shop. Sometimes the colour of wallpaper varies from roll to roll, but this should not happen if all the paper comes from the same batch number.

To check for colour variation, lay the rolls out overlapping each other, so that you can see at least 100 mm. (4 in.) of each, and look across the sheets.

If a colour does vary, arrange the sheets so that they run from dark to light.

If the colour in a roll varies from one side to the other, exchange the roll.

What you will need

Pasting table. You can make do with an ordinary kitchen table or make your own pasting table, 1800 × 600 mm. (6 × 2 ft).

Pasting brush. A 150 mm. (6 in.) distemper brush is best for applying the adhesive.

Hanging brush. Also known as a smoothing brush. It is used for smoothing the paper on to the wall. The better quality brushes are made of pure bristle which will not scratch the paper.

Scissors. A pair of 300 mm. (12 in.) paperhanger's scissors.

Plumb-line. Used for marking true verticals to align edges. You can make one from a length of string and a small weight.

Pasting bucket. Any sort of bucket that will hold a reasonable quantity of paste will do. Tie a piece of string across the top to rest the brush on when not in use.

Angle roller. A small boxwood roller used to run along butt-joins to ensure perfect adhesion—not an essential tool.

Sundries. Stripping knife; filling knife; glass-paper; sponge; pencil; trimming knife; clean cotton rags.

Adhesives

The type of paste you should use depends on the weight of the paper. The retailer will be able to advise you. It is better to use a paste that is too thick than one that is too thin.

Cellulose paste (Polycell etc.) is bought as a powder and mixed with water before use. It is good for light to medium-weight papers and has the advantage that it does not stain as badly as starch paste.

Cellulose paste is not suitable for some special papers, so check before using.

Starch/flour paste (Crown wallpaper adhesive etc.) is available in both the hot and cold water types. Both are more suitable for heavyweight papers than for the lighter and flimsier types.

Boxwood angle roller

Stripping knife

Trimming knife

Paste bucket

Pasting brush

300 mm. (12 in.) paperhanger's scissors

Plumb-line

Synthetic sponge

Hanging brush

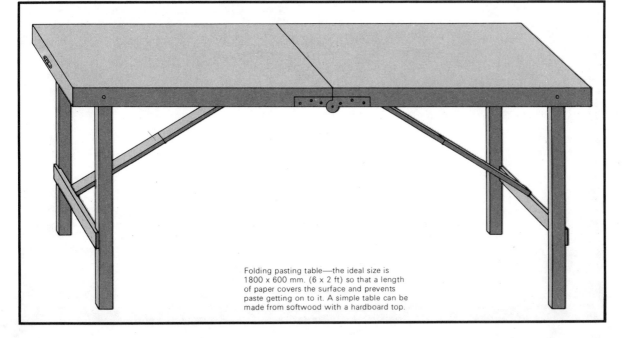

Folding pasting table—the ideal size is 1800 x 600 mm. (6 x 2 ft) so that a length of paper covers the surface and prevents paste getting on to it. A simple table can be made from softwood with a hardboard top.

Preparation

Surface treatment before papering

Previously papered surfaces. Strip the wall completely before repapering. Soak the paper several times with warm water or a stripping solution such as Polypeel. Apply the solution liberally, with an old distemper brush or cloth, until the paste is soft.

Scrape the paper off with a broad stripping knife, being careful not to dig it into the wall.

Score painted or varnished papers with a wire brush, soak and scrape off. Finally, wash off all traces of the old paste.

Remove paper from plasterboard with care—the water will damage the board if it has not been sealed.

Test a small patch first and, if it comes off satisfactorily, strip the rest of the wall. However, if the board becomes soft you will have to decorate over the old paper.

New plaster. If you move into a new house with undecorated plaster walls, ask the builder how long you must wait before you can decorate.

Some plasters must be left for at least six months before decorating; others can be painted or papered almost immediately.

Fill and size all plaster surfaces before hanging paper.

New plasterboard. Seal with primer to prevent water from softening the plaster when you come to strip the paper off. Hang lining paper as a backing for the final paper.

Emulsion painted surfaces. If the surface is sound and has a matt finish, sandpaper lightly and size. Add a small quantity of fine plaster to the size to give a key. Apply lining paper first if you are hanging heavy paper. Flaking emulsion must be stripped.

Oil painted surfaces. Rub down thoroughly with a pumice block or wet-or-dry paper and rinse off with clean water. Fill any cracks and hang lining paper. Gloss finishes must be stripped.

Sizing. Glue size prevents a wall from absorbing water from the paste too quickly and thus gives you time to reposition the paper you are hanging. Size is bought as a powder and mixed with water. Follow the instructions on the packet—if the size is too strong, it could make the wall so slippery that the paper would be unmanageable when put to the wall.

A coat of cellulose paste will also effectively seal a wall.

After sealing, allow the wall to dry, and sand it lightly before hanging the paper.

Lining paper. This can either be painted to help disguise a badly cracked wall or used as a backing for a final layer of paper.

Choose a lining paper of roughly the same colour as the final paper.

Hang lining paper horizontally and butt-join each sheet. Cut strips of paper to cover the length of the wall, fold the paper concertina-fashion, as with ceiling paper (p. 26), and start hanging it at the top of the wall.

Do not hang a continuous strip of paper round corners—take the paper up to a point 25 mm. (1 in.) round the corner, cut it off, and then butt-join the next strip.

Do not line the whole wall if only a small area is uneven. Hang lining paper over the damaged area, leave the ends hanging loose, and when the paste dries, tear them off. Sand the edges to remove any 'step'.

Stripping off old paper: soak liberally with warm water or a stripping solution.

Scrape off the paper with a stripping knife, taking care not to dig into the wall.

Hanging lining paper: fold the paper concertina-fashion, hang it horizontally.

Planning the order of work

Paper in the order shown here.

Start at a window and work towards the longest wall. Then return to the window and complete the remaining walls.

The chimney breast is the focal point of the room, and patterned papers must be centred on it, so hang the central roll first when you come to a chimney breast. This is not essential with striped or plain textured papers.

Matching, aligning and pasting

1. Cut the rolls of paper into lengths, making the first piece 100 mm. (4 in.) longer than the height of the wall to allow for trimming later.

The sheets will be butt-joined (laid side by side) when they are hung, so the pattern must be matched as you cut the lengths. After you have cut the first sheet, line the pattern up horizontally and cut the next to the same length as the first piece. Continue doing this until you have enough paper to cover the wall.

Remember that some odd lengths will fit over doors, windows, etc.

There will be more wastage when matching drop-patterned papers than in matching set patterns, but this cannot be avoided.

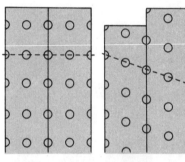

Set pattern   Drop pattern

2. To make sure that the paper is hung vertically you will need a plumb-line. Window-frames must not be used as verticals against which to align wallpaper: like door-frames and corners, they are likely to be slightly off the vertical.

Hang the first sheet of paper next to the brightest light source in the room, so that any slight overlap between adjoining sheets will not cast a shadow. This light source is usually a window.

To establish a true vertical, measure out from the window-frame a distance just under the width of the paper.

Suspend a plumb-line from this point and mark the wall at several points behind the line. Use a straight-edge to join them together.

3. Lay the bundle of cut sheets patterned side down on the pasting table with the ends overhanging each end of the table equally. Pull the top sheet into position ready for pasting by lining it up roughly with the back and side edges of the table. Both edges should overlap the table by about 5 mm. ($\frac{1}{8}-\frac{1}{4}$ in.).

Dip your brush in the paste to immerse about one-third of the bristles, and press it against the side of the paste bucket to remove any excess.

Divide the paper into three imaginary strips, and paste strip No. 1, the broad

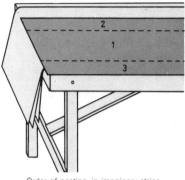

Order of pasting, in imaginary strips

central strip, first. Paste the outer strips from the centre outwards.

4. Paste strip No. 2, the one farthest away from you.

5. Pull the paper towards you, so that the near edge overhangs the bench by about 5 mm., and paste strip No. 3, the one nearest to you.

6. When you have pasted the first half of the top sheet, fold it over so the end rests on the centre and paste the other half. Loop this end over too when you have finished pasting it.

Arrange your work so that there is always a pasted piece soaking as you are hanging or pasting another sheet.

1. Match the pattern carefully as you cut lengths from the rolls of wallpaper.

2. Use a plumb-line near a window, to mark off a true vertical for the first sheet.

3. Divide the paper into three imaginary strips, and paste the central one first.

4. Paste the far strip next. It should overhang the pasting table very slightly.

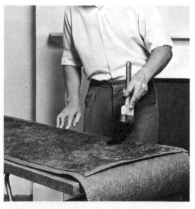

5. Pull the sheet to give a slight overhang at the front, and paste the front strip.

6. Fold over the pasted end and paste the other half of the sheet. (*continued*)

Papering walls/2

Hanging, trimming and turning corners

7. Carry the first looped sheet of paper, with the ends uppermost, to the wall. You will need to use a hop-up or small stepladder to reach the ceiling comfortably.

8. Unloop the top half of the sheet. Position the top of the paper against the ceiling, allowing an overlap for trimming, and lay its edge against the line you marked previously.

9. Run the hanging brush down the centre of the paper and work it towards the edges, to force out any air bubbles.

10. When you have finished the top half of the paper, unfurl the bottom and repeat the action with the hanging brush until the paper is smoothed on to the wall.

11. Run the back of the scissor blades along the edges of the ceiling and the skirting board, and along the window-frame if there is an overlap, to mark where the paper must be trimmed.

12. Peel the paper back slightly and trim off the surplus so that it fits neatly into place. Before placing the cut length back in position, sponge down the ceiling, skirting board and any other woodwork to remove excess paste. Then brush the paper back into position and smooth it down.

13. Place the next sheet of paper loosely on the wall, as close to the first sheet as possible. Slide it into position so that it forms an exact butt-join, and smooth and trim it in the same way as the first.

Be careful with thin papers, as they will tear easily if you slide them about too much.

14. Corners are often out of true, and if you try to hang a whole sheet of paper round a corner it will crease.

To prevent this, measure the distance from the last full width of paper to the corner in several places, add about 5 mm. ($\frac{1}{4}$ in.) to the largest of these measurements and cut a length of paper to this width.

Paste it up, hang it, and smooth it into place, with the extra 5 mm. extending round the corner.

15. Hang the remaining offcut so that it overlaps into the corner. Use a plumb-line to make sure that it is vertical. You will lose only 5 mm. of the pattern, and this will not be noticeable in the corner.

7. Carry the looped sheet to the wall, using a hop-up to reach ceiling height easily.

8. Position the paper overlapping the ceiling, and against the marked line.

9. Run the hanging brush down the centre of the sheet, and smooth out bubbles.

10. Unloop the bottom half of the sheet, and smooth it to the wall in the same way.

11. Mark top and bottom trimming-lines on the paper with the back of your scissors.

12. Peel the paper away and trim off the surplus before finally smoothing.

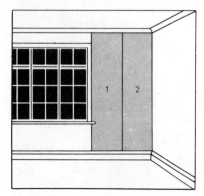

13. Butt-join the next sheet to the first, working away from the light source.

14. Do not hang a whole width round a corner: cut one to turn 5 mm. ($\frac{1}{4}$ in.).

15. Hang the remaining offcut so that it overlaps into the corner.

Chimney breasts, switches, awkward angles

16. The sheet of paper that goes above the fireplace, in the middle of the chimney breast, must be hung centrally if you are hanging a patterned paper, as this is the focal point of the room.

Hang this piece first, then work back to where you left off papering.

17. Take special care when you are trimming paper along the edges of the fireplace, as the weight of the paper may cause it to tear at its narrowest point, where it turns round the end of the mantelpiece. Avoid tugging the paper.

18. Trim the paper along the mantelpiece and remove as much waste as possible before smoothing it into place and cutting it to fit round the mouldings beneath the mantelpiece.

19. Allow a 25 mm. (1 in.) 'turn round' on projecting corners.

20. Before you paper round a light switch, turn the electricity off at the mains.

With projecting switches, press the knob through the paper and make a number of cuts in the shape of a star extending from the knob to approx. 20 mm. (¾ in.) past the edge of the switch mounting. This prevents the paper from tearing.

21. Trim off the waste and smooth the cut pieces back into place. At flush mounted switches, turn off the electricity, unscrew the cover plate and trim off the paper inside the switch cavity.

22. At large obstructions, such as door-frames, make a rough trimming-line by running the back of your scissors along the edge of the frame.

23. Cut along this line and press the paper into the angle before trimming off the remaining waste. Then smooth the paper back into position with your hanging brush.

24. When you come to windows, paper inside the recesses first, then overlap, as shown, to conceal the join.

16. At chimney breasts, start by hanging a sheet of wallpaper centrally.

17. Mark a line for trimming along the mantelpiece. Avoid tugging the paper.

18. Trim off as much waste as possible before fitting paper beneath the mantel.

19. Allow a 25 mm. (1 in.) 'turn round' on projecting corners at chimney breasts etc.

20. At light switches, make a series of cuts to form a star shape.

21. Trim off the waste and smooth the paper back into place around the switch.

22. At door-frames, make a rough trimming-line with the back of your scissors.

23. After the final trimming round doors, smooth the paper, pressing into the angle.

24. Hang paper inside window recesses, then overlap to conceal the join.

Papering ceilings

Equipment and procedure

Papering a ceiling is a difficult job. If you can get away with just painting a ceiling, then do so.

But if you must paper, arrange a platform, using two step-ladders and a plank, so that you can cover the full width of the ceiling without having to get down. Your head should be approximately 150 mm. (6 in.) below the ceiling.

If you have no platform, you will have to use a special adjustable pole to hold the paper up. This pole is spring-loaded and has a platform at the top to support the paper, leaving you with both hands free.

1. Hang the paper across the ceiling. Start working by the window and continue hanging towards the back of the room. Chalk a guide line on the ceiling to help you lay the first strip accurately.

2. Cut the paper into lengths, allowing a slight overlap for trimming at the ends of each piece, until you have sufficient pieces to cover the ceiling. Paste up in the same way as for wallpaper (p. 23) and fold the paper concertina-fashion.

3. Using part of a spare roll to support the paper from underneath, start sticking it up. Unfurl it one fold at a time, smoothing it on to the ceiling with a brush.

Butt-join each new sheet to the last as you cover the ceiling in this way.

4. Make star-shaped cuts round light fittings in the same way as for projecting wall switches (p. 25). Fit the paper into place and, after the length has been completed, trim the waste off neatly.

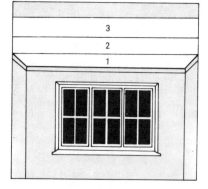

1. Hang the paper across the ceiling, working back from the window.

2. When the paper has been pasted, fold it concertina-fashion, ready for fixing.

3. As you unfold the paper and smooth it on, support the rest with a spare roll.

4. Make star cuts round light fittings and trim after completing the length.

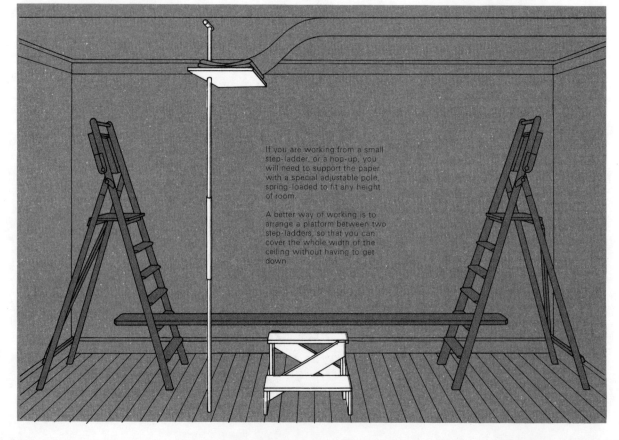

If you are working from a small step-ladder, or a hop-up, you will need to support the paper with a special adjustable pole, spring-loaded to fit any height of room.

A better way of working is to arrange a platform between two step-ladders, so that you can cover the whole width of the ceiling without having to get down.

The secret—a safe working-platform

Take up the stair carpets and arrange a scaffolding system with ladders and planks, so that you have easy access to both the head wall and the well wall. Make sure that the ladders are perfectly secure. If the boards are longer than 1·5 m. (5 ft) from support to support, place one board on top of another for strength.

Use a plumb-line to establish a true vertical on the well wall, and hang the first length of paper at the corner so that about 10 mm. (½ in.) turns on to the head wall.

The weight of the paste will stretch, and may even tear, the long pieces of paper. Get someone to stand below and support the weight as much as possible.

When you have finished papering the well wall, remove the scaffold board and complete the head wall, working from a ladder set on the main landing.

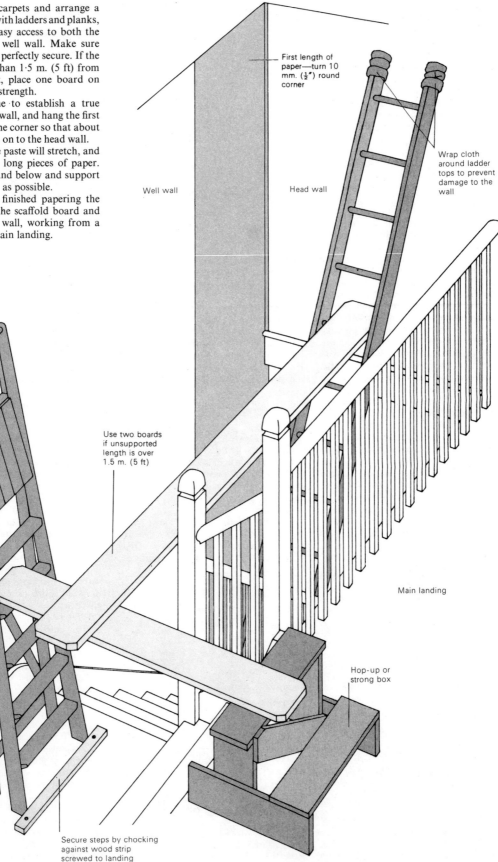

First length of paper—turn 10 mm. (½") round corner

Wrap cloth around ladder tops to prevent damage to the wall

Well wall

Head wall

Use two boards if unsupported length is over 1.5 m. (5 ft)

Main landing

Hop-up or strong box

Secure steps by chocking against wood strip screwed to landing

Hanging unusual materials

Hessian, felt, Anaglypta and vinyl

Hessian can be bought either specially prepared for hanging on walls or as ordinary furnishing hessian.

Prepared hessian is backed, usually with paper, latex or foam, and is easier to handle than furnishing hessian. It is sold in 915 mm. (36 in.) widths in a wide range of colours as well as for painting.

Furnishing hessian is quite suitable for hanging on walls. It is sold in 915 mm. and 1270 mm. (50 in.) widths and is about half the price of backed hessian. It will not obscure sharp differences in colour on the wall, so first hang coloured lining paper on patchy walls.

Furnishing hessian can be painted, preferably with thin oil paint.

Before you hang hessian, the wall must be clean, so strip off any existing wallpaper. Prepare the wall as for wallpaper.

Start at a corner and measure off a distance 25 mm. (1 in.) less than the width of the hessian. Using a plumb-line, chalk a vertical line on the wall at this point. Measure the height of the wall, add 50 mm. (2 in.) for shrinkage in furnishing hessian and cut the strip to length.

The manufacturers of prepared hessian recommend suitable adhesives and how to apply them: hang furnishing hessian with heavy-duty wallpaper paste applied to the wall and evened out with a roller.

Prepared hessian is hung and butt-joined in the same way as wallpaper, but a different procedure is needed for a neat join in furnishing hessian.

Centre the piece of hessian, with one edge on the chalk line and a 25 mm. overlap on the other three edges.

Starting from the top of the wall, pat the hessian down gently with your hand and work towards the bottom. Smooth the fabric down finally with a clean paint roller, working from the centre.

Hang other strips to overlap the previous strip by about 25 mm.

Do not do anything about the joins until all the hessian is up and the adhesive has dried—there is certain to be some shrinkage. If you get some adhesive on the surface of the hessian, wipe it off with a cloth before it has a chance to dry.

When hanging furnishing hessian, do not distort the weave too much.

To butt-join the pieces, you need a sharp knife and a straight-edge. Cut through both thicknesses at the overlap, peel back the edges and remove the waste.

Apply more paste to the wall under the flaps and press the edges into place.

Decorative felt is available in more than 60 colours. It is sold in 1829 mm. (72 in.) wide rolls by department stores. The problem in hanging felt is its weight.

You can overcome this by: (a) dividing the felt into narrower strips (this makes it more manageable, but it also increases the number of joins); or (b) supporting it on a batten while you hang it.

To support felt, cut a strip the height of the wall, with a 50 mm. allowance for shrinkage, and roll it on to a batten. Apply the adhesive (e.g. Clam 143) to the wall.

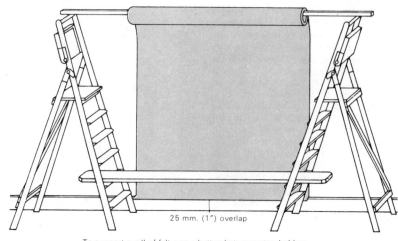

25 mm. (1") overlap

To support a roll of felt, use a batten between step-ladders.

Get somebody to hold the roll, or support it on steps, so that the fabric is parallel to the wall. Press the felt to the wall from the bottom up, and smooth it with a paint roller. Allow 25 mm. overlaps and cut the joins as for hessian, then tease the edges to hide the join.

Anaglypta is hung after the surface has been prepared in the same way as for ordinary wallpaper, then rubbed down with abrasive paper to provide a key.

If the wall is in a bad condition, fill in cracks then hang lining paper, using a starch/flour paste. Use Ready Mixed Dextrine paste to glue on Anaglypta. Dampen the back of panels lightly with a sponge and put them to one side for 10–15 minutes before pasting. This makes them more supple and less springy.

Apply the paste with a small trowel to those parts of the panel that will come into contact with the wall. Use pins to hold the panels in position until the adhesive dries, and remove them afterwards.

Use Dextrine paste again to attach Anaglypta decorations to the wall. Spread the paste on the edges of the decorations and press them into place. Use panel pins to hold the decorations in place until the glue dries.

Hang low-relief Anaglypta in the same way as other papers. Use a thick starch paste and allow the paper to soak for 5 minutes before you hang it. Smooth carefully, so as not to damage the relief effect.

Anaglypta must be painted after it is hung, preferably with emulsion paint. Once painted, it can be washed without it coming away.

Vinyl must be hung with a paste that contains a fungicide (Crown Vinyl adhesive etc.) to prevent mould from growing under the paper. Prepare the wall in the same way as for ordinary papers. Apply the paste to the back of the vinyl and hang it immediately; it does not need to be left to soak.

The edges must be butt-joined, as any overlap will not stick to the surface of the vinyl. If you cannot avoid an overlap as you hang the vinyl, use the same technique as for butt-joining hessian.

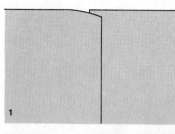

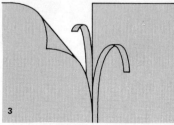

Furnishing hessian: 1. Allow a 25 mm. (1 in.) overlap as you hang each new piece. 2. Cut through both pieces at the centre of the overlap, using a sharp knife and a straight-edge. 3. Remove waste strips. 4. Paste the wall then press hessian into place.

A quick, neat way of redecorating

Polystyrene tiles provide an effective method of covering cracked or discoloured ceilings. Do not use them where there is any risk of their becoming overheated (near fireplaces or above gas water heaters). They should never be painted.

Most ceiling tiles measure 305 × 305 × 9 mm. (12 × 12 × ⅜ in.), but 610 × 610 mm. (2 × 2 ft) and 229 × 229 mm. (9 × 9 in.) sizes are also available and some are only 6 mm. (¼ in.) thick.

Remove polystyrene tiles which have been painted over with gloss paint—they constitute a great fire risk.

Adhesives. Special adhesives are sold for fixing polystyrene tiles, but not all are suitable for every surface to be covered. For instance, Marley No. 124 can be used on emulsion-painted ceilings, but Evo-stik 863 is unsuitable.

Preparing the surface. Make good cracked ceilings and remove and replace any loose plaster. Hair-line cracks need no attention. Remove distemper with water and sponge. Wash emulsion paint. Rub over gloss paint with glasspaper or a wire brush to provide a good key for the adhesive. Remove any traces of grease with a liquid detergent. If the grease is thick, use Flash or liquid Ajax.

On really rough ceilings, remove all the existing plaster and laths, then face the joists with standard or medium hard-board, and fix the tiles to that.

Marking up. Draw lines dividing ceiling in half along the length and the width [1]. Measure lines AB and AC, and count the number of whole tiles that will go along each line.

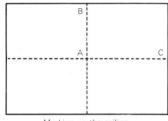

Marking up the ceiling.

If the space left over is 152 mm. (6 in.) or more (i.e. at least half a tile), you can fix the tiles from the marked line. If it is less than 152 mm., you would end up with a narrow, unsightly row of tiles near the wall, so mark a new line 152 mm. from the centre line and work from that.

If there is a central light fitting, cut the corners of the four centre tiles with a sharp trimming knife to fit snugly round the rose, using a conveniently sized cup as a guide.

If the rose is offset, or the centre lines do not intersect at this point, adjust one of the centre lines so that the rose comes between rows of tiles. Cut semicircles in adjacent tiles to fit round it.

If the ceiling has a tubular light fitting,

arrange its centre line to fall between two rows of tiles. You may have to re-align the fitting, because it should at least lie parallel to these rows.

All tiles which butt on to the fitting will have to be cut to fit round it snugly.

Fixing. Recent findings by fire authorities recommend fixing polystyrene tiles with an even coat of adhesive, which excludes air pockets behind them. Spread a 1·5 mm. (1/16 in.) thick layer of adhesive in one of the right angles formed by the centre lines and over an area large enough to take about nine tiles. Firm the tiles with a flat block to avoid making finger dents [2].

Fix tiles in the remaining three angles, to form a square at the centre, and continue tiling outwards. If there is a large central obstruction, the ceiling can be tiled in two separate sections.

Check constantly that the tiles fit closely together and run in straight lines [3].

To mark border tiles for cutting, place a 'dry' tile over the last fixed tile [4]. Hold a third tile as shown, one edge against the wall, and mark with a pencil where it overlaps the 'dry' tile. The part of the tile that remains uncovered will fit the border exactly when cut [5].

Polystyrene cove, available in several sizes, is fixed with the same adhesive as tiles [6]. Fix the corner mitres first—they can be bought pre-cut. Cove improves the decorative effect and conceals narrow borders.

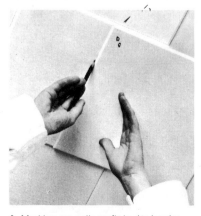

1. Marking up centre lines on the ceiling.

2. Firming the first tile in place with a pad.

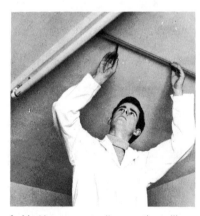

3. Fit tiles close together as you proceed.

4. Marking up a tile to fit in the border.

5. Cutting a border tile to a marked line.

6. Finishing with polystyrene cove.

Tongued and grooved panelling

How to line walls with timber

Interlocking tongued and grooved boards can be fixed to any type of wall. Vertical boards tend to make a room look higher, horizontal boards longer.

Screw or nail 50 × 25 mm. (2 × 1 in.) timber battens to the wall, in the opposite direction to the run of the boarding, to provide the base for fixing the boards.

If the plaster is sound and not too thick, masonry nails provide the quickest method of securing the battens. First drive the nails into a batten, then hold the batten against the wall and drive the nails home. If the plaster is thick or crumbly, fasten the battens with screws and wallplugs.

Fix the battens 400 mm. (16 in.) apart, at least up to shoulder height. Above this level the spacing can be increased to 600–900 mm. (2–3 ft).

Remove existing architraves from around door and window openings and fasten battens in their place. Remove skirting boards. If the walls tend to be damp, treat the battens with wood preservative and sandwich building paper between the wall and battens.

Bring the front surfaces of the battens to a uniform vertical plane by inserting plywood or hardboard packing behind them.

A nominal 100 mm. wide tongued and grooved board covers only 85 mm. (3½ in.) when interlocked. A wall 3500 mm. (12 ft) long and 2500 mm. (8 ft) high requires just under 43 boards, each 2500 mm. long: i.e., 108 m. It would be advisable to order at least 115 m. to allow for waste.

When fastening boards upright, start from a corner. Pin the first board up and check that the edge further from the corner is vertical. Repeat on the other arm of the corner, planing the inside edge of the second board so that it butts neatly.

Interlock the boarding as tightly as possible, since it is bound to shrink considerably during initial drying. Fasten with secret nails through the tongues into the battens. Alternatively, nail through the boards, punch the heads and fill the holes with plastic wood.

To fit a board ceiling, fix the boards directly to the joists with 40 mm. (1½ in.) pins. Butt-joint boards for long spans, centring joints beneath a joist. Short lengths must cover at least two joists. Do not let joints in adjacent boards coincide.

Clad existing ceilings, provided laths are free from woodworm, by fixing through the plaster into the joists. Locate the joists by drilling small holes through the plaster at each side of the room and ruling in the centre lines. If boards are to run in line with the joists, fix battens at 90° to the joists with 60 mm. (2½ in.) cut nails, and pin the boards to the battens.

At electrical sockets and light switches, re-route the existing wiring into new metal mounting boxes surrounded by a framework of battens. Stop the boards so that switch and socket plates cover the ends.

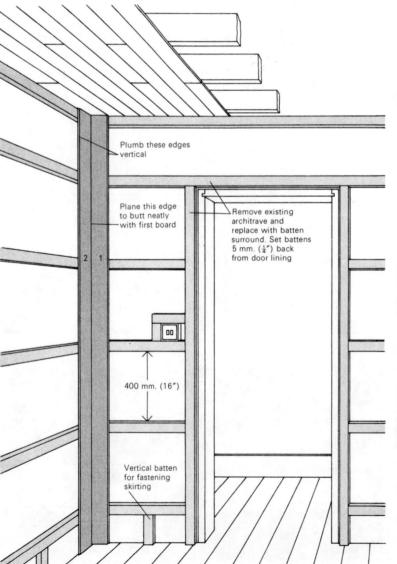

Plumb these edges vertical

Plane this edge to butt neatly with first board

Remove existing architrave and replace with batten surround. Set battens 5 mm. (¼″) back from door lining

400 mm. (16″)

Vertical batten for fastening skirting

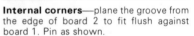

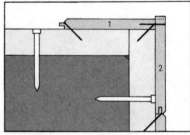

Internal corners—plane the groove from the edge of board 2 to fit flush against board 1. Pin as shown.

External corners—trim board 1 to line up with face of battens on return wall. Saw groove or tongue off board 2. Pin board 2 in place and plane off slight overlap.

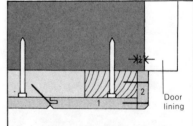

Door-frames—nail vertical batten 5 mm. (¼ in.) back from edge of door lining, and horizontal batten 5 mm. up from top edge. Line the wall, finishing with board 1 cut flush with edge of batten. Cut board 2 to fit tightly between the door lining and board 1.

Choosing plastic and cork tiles

Vinyl-tiled floors are especially suitable for kitchens and bathrooms. They are hard-wearing and resistant to grease and acids. **Vinyl and vinyl asbestos tiles** have different uses. Choose vinyl asbestos for a solid floor if you are uncertain whether or not it has a damp-proof membrane; a floor with the slightest trace of damp is unsuitable for laying vinyl tiles, whereas vinyl asbestos will tolerate some damp.

Both types can be laid on suspended timber floors, provided the underfloor ventilation is really good. Do not lay tiles on timber treated with a preservative, on bituminous underfelts or directly on new boards, which may shrink. Prepare uneven floors as for laying sheet vinyl (p. 34).

Vinyl asbestos tiles are more brittle than vinyl tiles; store them in a warm room before laying, or place them near a fan heater, to increase their flexibility. As colours may vary slightly between batches, mix the contents of different boxes before starting work. Lay the tiles glossy side up and with the grain or marbling on adjacent tiles running in opposite directions.

Special adhesive, such as Evo-stik 426, is needed for laying floor tiles. Follow the instructions on the tin.

There are also self-adhesive tiles which have a coating of glue and a backing sheet of greaseproof paper. With the paper peeled away, the tile is pressed in place.

Lift old or unwanted tiles with a sharp scraper, heating the top gently with a blow-torch if you have one. If an odd tile comes loose, scrape away the old adhesive and remove loose dust before applying a fresh coating and replacing the tile. To remove dried adhesive or paint from tiles, rub with a cloth dipped in white spirit, cleaning quickly as the spirit dissolves vinyl.

For a long-lasting, non-slip surface, apply a plastic sealant, such as Marley Clearseal, after carefully cleaning the newly laid tiles. For a high gloss finish, apply a water-based emulsion wax polish. **Cork tiles** are laid in much the same way as vinyl tiles. They require a firm, level surface and it is essential for solid floors to have a damp-proof membrane. Prepare cracked or uneven floors as for sheet vinyl (p. 34).

Cover suspended timber floors with sheets of seasoned hardboard, staggering the sheets to avoid continuous joints. Good underfloor ventilation is essential.

Some vinyl tile adhesives are suitable for cork tiles; a special adhesive is sold by the Armstrong Cork Co. Additionally, cork tiles are held down by driving in five headless pins, one at each corner and one in the centre. On hard surfaces, weigh the tiles down with bags filled with sand, or other heavy objects, until the glue sets.

Tile manufacturers supply concentrated polishes for a hard wax finish; this can be maintained with wax polish or plastic sealants.

Estimating and planning

Vinyl and vinyl asbestos tiles, which are generally 250 × 250 mm. (10 × 10 in.) and 229 × 229 mm. (9 × 9 in.), are available in a variety of colours, mostly marbled. If you propose using two colours, plan a pattern for laying before you start work. Cork tiles are 300 × 300 mm. or 12 × 12 in. and are sold in various shades.

To estimate the quantity needed when buying plastic tiles of one colour only, first measure the length and breadth of the room. Using the chart alongside, follow the lines from these measurements to the point of intersection, then read off the total number of tiles required. For instance, you will need 252 tiles for a room 4·5 × 3·5 m. or 13 × 10 ft. If a hearth protrudes, measure this separately and subtract the appropriate number of tiles.

Divide irregularly shaped rooms into rectangles, estimate the number of tiles needed for each, and add those numbers together for the total required.

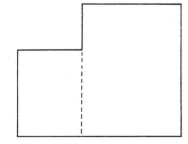

Divide odd shapes into rectangles

If tiles of two colours are to be laid chequer-board fashion or in alternate rows, simply halve the total and buy equal quantities of each colour. For more complex patterns, trace a scale plan of the room from the chart, drawing in the lines of tiles but omitting the numbers. Shade in the pattern and count up the number of tiles needed of each colour.

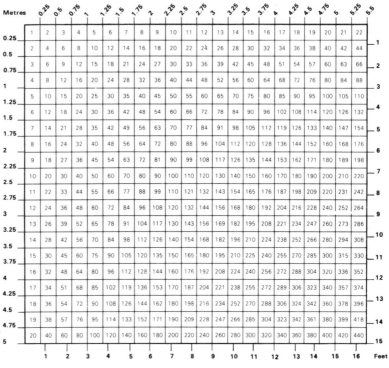

Metres	0.25	0.5	0.75	1	1.25	1.5	1.75	2	2.25	2.5	2.75	3	3.25	3.5	3.75	4	4.25	4.5	4.75	5	5.25	5.5	Feet
0.25	1	2	3	4	5	6	7	8	9	10	11	12	13	14	15	16	17	18	19	20	21	22	
0.5	2	4	6	8	10	12	14	16	18	20	22	24	26	28	30	32	34	36	38	40	42	44	1
0.75	3	6	9	12	15	18	21	24	27	30	33	36	39	42	45	48	51	54	57	60	63	66	2
1	4	8	12	16	20	24	28	32	36	40	44	48	52	56	60	64	68	72	76	80	84	88	3
1.25	5	10	15	20	25	30	35	40	45	50	55	60	65	70	75	80	85	90	95	100	105	110	4
1.5	6	12	18	24	30	36	42	48	54	60	66	72	78	84	90	96	102	108	114	120	126	132	
1.75	7	14	21	28	35	42	49	56	63	70	77	84	91	98	105	112	119	126	133	140	147	154	5
2	8	16	24	32	40	48	56	64	72	80	88	96	104	112	120	128	136	144	152	160	168	176	6
2.25	9	18	27	36	45	54	63	72	81	90	99	108	117	126	135	144	153	162	171	180	189	198	7
2.5	10	20	30	40	50	60	70	80	90	100	110	120	130	140	150	160	170	180	190	200	210	220	
2.75	11	22	33	44	55	66	77	88	99	110	121	132	143	154	165	176	187	198	209	220	231	242	8
3	12	24	36	48	60	72	84	96	108	120	132	144	156	168	180	192	204	216	228	240	252	264	9
3.25	13	26	39	52	65	78	91	104	117	130	143	156	169	182	195	208	221	234	247	260	273	286	
3.5	14	28	42	56	70	84	98	112	126	140	154	168	182	196	210	224	238	252	266	280	294	308	10
3.75	15	30	45	60	75	90	105	120	135	150	165	180	195	210	225	240	255	270	285	300	315	330	11
4	16	32	48	64	80	96	112	128	144	160	176	192	208	224	240	256	272	288	304	320	336	352	12
4.25	17	34	51	68	85	102	119	136	153	170	187	204	221	238	255	272	289	306	323	340	357	374	
4.5	18	36	54	72	90	108	126	144	162	180	198	216	234	252	270	288	306	324	342	360	378	396	13
4.75	19	38	57	76	95	114	133	152	171	190	209	228	247	266	285	304	323	342	361	380	399	418	14
5	20	40	60	80	100	120	140	160	180	200	220	240	260	280	300	320	340	360	380	400	420	440	15
	1	2	3	4	5	6	7	8	9	10	11	12	13	14	15	16							Feet

How many tiles? Read the top and left-hand side of the table for metric measurements and metric tiles, the bottom and right-hand side for imperial. Add 6–12, according to the total, for wastage to the metric total and the same to any imperial total for an area that is an exact multiple of nine, i.e., 6 × 12, 9 × 9 or 15 × 12 ft.

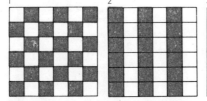
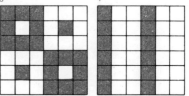

Patterns need varying ratios of different coloured tiles: patterns 1–3 need half the total in each colour; pattern 4 one-third in one colour and two-thirds in the other.

Laying floor tiles/1

Marking out; spreading adhesive

Rub a line with chalk and tie it between the pins A and B, which are tacked into the floor or skirting in the middle of facing walls [1]. Position the pins about 25 mm. (1 in.) above the level of the floor.

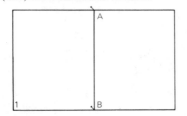

Check that the line is taut, then snap it to leave a chalk mark on the floor. Remove the lines but leave the pins [2].

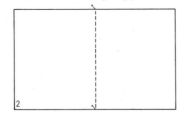

Mark the centre of the chalk line and run a row of 'dry' tiles to a side wall, lining the first tile up with the chalk line and the centre mark [3].

If the gap between the last tile and the side wall is 75 mm. (3 in.) or less, move the whole row 125 mm. (4½ in.) away from the wall. This will give adequate borders, of equal width, against the side walls. Snap a fresh line on the floor [4].

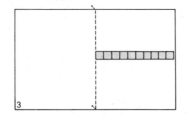

If the gap is more than 75 mm. wide, or after you have marked the new line, run another row of tiles at right angles to the first one [5].

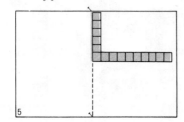

Snapping a chalked line. On long lengths, press the centre of the string on the floor and snap each side in turn. Any light-coloured powder will do instead of chalk.

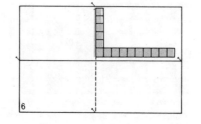

Measuring the gap between the last of a row of 'dry' tiles and the wall.

Again, if the gap between the new row and the wall is 75 mm. or less, move both rows of tiles 125 mm. back and snap a chalk line at right angles to the first [6].

For a wider border, set the row 125 mm. away from the wall and snap a new line.

You have now established the lines against which to lay the tiles. With the pins in place, spread adhesive over the lines and snap fresh chalk lines on top when set [7].

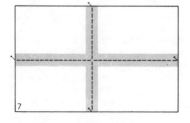

Covering the floor; tackling borders

Tile half the room at a time, first spreading adhesive over about 1 sq. m. (1 sq. yd) of floor on each side of the centre line. Place the first two tiles in the right angles of the chalk lines, then work outwards from each side to form a pyramid pattern. Spread more adhesive and continue tiling up to the borders.

Next cut border tiles: place a 'dry' tile exactly over an adjacent 'fixed' tile, hold another on top, flush with the wall, and score along the inner edge. The trimmed section A will fit the border [8].

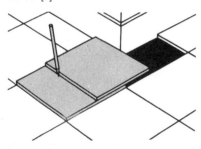

8. Cutting a border tile

Use the same method when cutting a tile to fit an angle, such as a door-frame or chimney breast. First, place and mark the tile as though cutting it for a straight border [9].

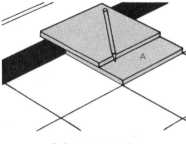

9. Cutting to an angle—stage 1

Move the tile, without turning it, opposite the other face of the angle, again placing it over a fixed tile, and draw a line at right angles to intersect the first [10]. Cut along the lines up to the intersection with a knife or pair of scissors.

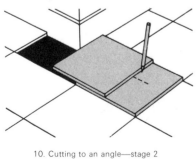

10. Cutting to an angle—stage 2

Treat more complicated shapes, such as curved architraves, in the same way, but taking separate measurements from each surface in both tile positions. In example [11], with the tile in its first position, draw lines a tile-width away from the sur-

Lay the tiles outwards to cover a pyramid-shaped area, starting with tiles 1 and 2 against the lines. Where you can, kneel on the tiles as you work.

Butt each tile against the adjacent ones, lowering it into place rather than sliding it.

Use a knife to scribe border tiles, then bend the tile to complete the break.

faces A, B, C and D. Where the outline is curved, draw a freehand cutting line between marks after making intersections from the second tile position.

In practice, this method of marking is easier than it sounds and perfectly accurate. If you prefer, cut paper templates of corners or irregular shapes; or shape a length of soft wire to the outline and transfer this to the tile as a tracing guide. You can buy adjustable template formers. These consist of a row of movable needles which take the shape of any object they are pushed against.

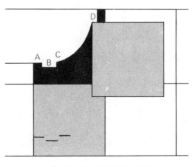

11. Cutting a complicated shape

Sheet floor-covering

Sheet vinyl, which has largely replaced linoleum, is available in a range of colours and designs and is suitable for covering any floor that is dry, smooth and firm.

It is unsuitable for solid floors that do not have a damp-proof membrane; before laying vinyl on a suspended timber floor, check that airbricks round the outside of the house are fully exposed and unblocked.

Improve cracked or uneven concrete floors by filling small holes with cement or plaster or by laying a self-smoothing screed (see opposite page). In timber floors,

fasten loose boards and, if necessary, level with a plane or sanding machine.

As an alternative to sanding, lay sheets of 4 mm. resin-bonded plywood, securing these with screws or with annular nails, spaced about 150 mm. (6 in.) apart, and staggering the sheets to avoid continuous joints. Leave 3 mm. ($\frac{1}{8}$ in.) expansion gaps between sheets.

Hardboard, which is cheaper than plywood, can be used instead if the underfloor ventilation is really efficient. Hardboard is absorbent and will bend to the

shape of the boards beneath if it becomes damp. Condition it before use and lay it rough side up.

Sheet vinyl is in several widths, up to a maximum of 1830 mm. (6 ft). Before choosing, decide which way the floor-covering is to run, avoiding joins at doorways. Store vinyl at room temperature for a day or so before laying.

For laying the vinyl you need a scriber, made by hammering a nail through a batten, 150 mm. (6 in.) from one end, so that the point protrudes 3 mm.

Laying step by step

Cut from the roll a sheet of vinyl 25–50 mm. (1–2 in.) longer than the length of the room. Lay it parallel with, and about 125 mm. (5 in.) from, a side wall, with the ends riding up on each end wall.

Holding the scriber at right angles to the side wall, with one end pressing against the skirting, make a continuous scratch line close to the edge of the vinyl [1]. Cut or pull off the surplus vinyl, then move the sheet to fit flush against the wall.

Lay subsequent lengths of vinyl to overlap the first by 25 mm., roughly trimming where necessary to fit the outline of bays, chimney breasts and other irregular shapes. The ends should again ride up an inch or two on each end wall [2].

Use a Stanley knife or sharp scissors to cut off the lengths of vinyl and also for subsequent trimming. Leave the vinyl to settle for a fortnight or so before trimming. It can be walked on during this time.

When the vinyl has settled, check that the scribed edges are flush with the skirting, moving the outside sheets if necessary. Using a straight-edge, cut through the mid point of the overlap between sheets [3], peel off the surplus and butt the sheets together.

Fix double-sided tape to the floor under each joint (the floor must be dust-free) to prevent the edges being kicked up.

All that remains is to trim the ends, which will now appear to have shrunk.

This is simple but involves several stages: first, make a pencil mark on one edge of the sheet [4] at a convenient distance from the skirting—say, 250 mm. (9 in.).

Draw the sheet back from the wall so that it lies flat, with the excess riding up the other end wall. Then measure the same distance (250 mm.) from your mark towards the end of the sheet, making a second mark at this point [5].

Adjust the sheet so that the nail on your scriber corresponds with this second mark, then scribe along the end, with the end of the scriber against the skirting board and the edge of the sheet flush with the adjacent sheet [6]. Follow the same procedure for cutting round corners and angles.

1. The first sheet; using a scriber to mark a line parallel with the side wall.

2. Overlapping the sheets. Surplus against the end wall is trimmed later.

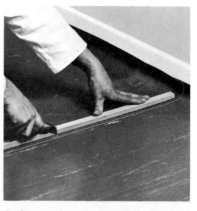

3. Cutting through the overlap between sheets, after the vinyl has settled.

4. Making a pencil mark 250 mm. (9 in.) from the end skirting, in readiness for trimming.

5. Making a second mark, nearer the end of the sheet, 250 mm. from the first.

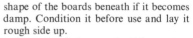

6. Scribing along the end of the sheet, starting at the second pencil mark.

Wood and solid floors

Laying wood blocks and strip flooring

Modern types of parquet and wood strip flooring are easier to lay and much cheaper than the traditional thick hardwood blocks. There are a number of different patterns and methods of fixing, with timber thicknesses of 2·5–9 mm. ($\frac{1}{10}$–$\frac{3}{8}$ in.). All have a long life: 50 years or more is claimed by the manufacturers.

Thinner types of flooring need a completely smooth, level sub-floor. Slight unevenness is acceptable with some of the thicker types, particularly when a cork underlay is used. Manufacturers' instructions specify the quality of sub-floor needed.

The simplest wood flooring is made up of plywood squares, which can be laid diagonally or with the grain forming a chequer-board pattern. An extension of this idea is the mosaic block, in which several parallel strips of hardwood are mounted on a single backing sheet. There are also mosaics in which fingers of hardwood make up a basket-weave pattern in a panel 457 × 457 mm. (18 × 18 in.).

Individual fingers are available for simulating traditional herringbone and brick-bond parquet patterns; also longer strips, about 75 mm. (3 in.) wide, for laying as wood strip flooring.

There are three main methods of fastening parquet panels and strip flooring:
1. Panel pins can be used on strip flooring, when there is a wooden sub-floor. The pins are driven diagonally through the tongued face on each strip or through interlocking ears which protrude from the side of the strip.
2. Adhesives can be used for fixing blocks and strips of all types on solid floors. The type of adhesive that is most effective is recommended by the manufacturer in leaflets which come with the flooring. Several manufacturers supply bitumen-based adhesives; others recommend contact adhesives, which must be applied to both the floor and the underside of the tiles. Some parquet blocks are supplied ready-coated with contact adhesive, so that only the sub-floor needs treating.
3. Interlocking panels can be laid without fastenings of any kind, except for the last few panels, which must be glued to those already laid, and cut to size if need be.

Some parquets are given a gloss finish by the manufacturers; others are supplied sanded but unsealed. Though the former entail less work, it is essential to lay the components absolutely level, as further sanding will spoil the finish. Untreated blocks can be given a final sanding after laying to ensure a perfectly smooth surface, then given two coats of floor sealer, such as Ronseal, before polishing. Alternatively, they can be treated with transparent lacquer, supplied by the parquet manufacturers.

Wood strip flooring (Par-K-Ply) is secured with panel pins pushed through interlocking ears on the sides of the strips. Use adhesives, not pins, on solid floors.

How to get a smooth solid floor

Self-smoothing screeds or underlayments, such as Ardit Z8 and Plycolay, are an easy method of preparing uneven concrete or quarry-tiled floors before laying tiles, sheet vinyl, wood blocks or parquet panels. The material is poured on to the floor and levelled roughly with a steel trowel, after which it spreads out by itself to form a smooth surface.

It is intended to correct only minor irregularities and is unsuitable for floors affected significantly by rising damp—such as brick floors laid directly on earth —or for covering suspended timber floors or wood block floors. If there is the slightest risk of damp, use vinyl asbestos tiles (which 'breathe') rather than vinyl; do not lay wood block floors.

Before applying the screed, wash the floor with detergent to remove grease and polish; sweep away loose dirt. When applied to absorbent surfaces, such as concrete, the screed can be walked on in an hour or so and the floor covering laid next day. Drying takes up to 24 hours on non-absorbent undersurfaces, such as quarry tiles.

Prime non-absorbent surfaces, such as quarry tiles, with an adhesive primer (e.g. Ardex Neoprene or Isobond). Dampen absorbent surfaces with water.

Mix the powder with water. Stir the mixture into a creamy paste, then pour part of it on to the floor at the furthest point from the door.

Spread the material evenly over the floor, using a steel trowel, to an average thickness of 3 mm. ($\frac{1}{8}$ in.). The self-smoothing action removes trowel marks.

Ceramic tiles/1

Types

Do-it-yourself ceramic tiling has become so popular that manufacturers now produce a range of tiles specially for this market. Most of them have spacer lugs on the edges so that they can be spaced accurately on the wall. They are available with surface finishes that are plain, patterned or textured.

Plain tiles are available in some ten colours. Most manufacturers' ranges include blue, yellow, green, grey, mauve, pink, black and white—colours designed to match the most popular colours in sanitary ware.

Textured tiles are produced in the same range of colours as plain tiles and most manufacturers offer a choice of two or three different textured effects. These textured tiles can be used on their own or interspersed in an area of plain tiling.

Patterned tiles are usually silk screen printed and all manufacturers have a large range of stock patterns. These tiles are not usually stocked by retail stores.

Transfer tiles, with illustrations of cars, ships, fish, etc., are available on request.

Apart from the do-it-yourself tiles, there is a larger range produced for the building industry. These tiles are more expensive than the do-it-yourself type, but the variety of colours, patterns and embossed effects is much larger.

Details of these tiles can be obtained direct from the manufacturers or through a builders' merchant.

Special-purpose tiles

Heat-resistant tiles are for use on the surrounds of fireplaces and on areas adjacent to solid fuel cookers where the surface temperature can rise to over 150°C (302°F).

In most cases, the thinner tile is adequate up to that temperature. Above it, the thicker tile will offer better resistance and withstand cracking. These heat-resistant tiles do not all have spacer lugs—sticks must be used to ensure correct spacing of tiles not made with lugs.

Frost-resistant tiles are for use in areas where the temperature is likely to fall below freezing point. They are essential for all exterior work.

Any tiles can be treated to render them frost-resistant, but this can be done only at the factory. The process increases the cost of tiles by approx. £1 per sq. m.

Sizes and sections

The table below shows the range of tiles normally used for do-it-yourself work. The smaller tiles are the more readily available and are more commonly used.

The measurements of 100 and 200 mm. tiles are inclusive of the joint widths.

Tiles can be obtained from builders' merchants and tile specialists or direct from the factory. Pamphlets showing ranges of sizes and colours can usually be obtained direct from manufacturers.

Only three different tile sections will be required for do-it-yourself jobs: field tiles, RE tiles (one rounded edge), and REX tiles (two rounded edges).

Field tiles. These will be used on the bulk of the area to be covered. They have square-set edges, and most have spacer lugs for accurate spacing when laying.

Some special purpose field tiles have no spacer lugs, and they must be spaced by the use of sticks in the joints.

RE tiles. These have one rounded edge and are used for finishing off the edges of the tiled area. Manufacturing difficulties prevent these tiles from being made with spacer lugs.

REX tiles. These have two rounded adjacent edges and are used to finish off the corner of a tiled area. They also are made without spacer lugs.

	Uses	Sizes	Finish	Lugs
WALL TILES	General purpose	108 × 108 × 4 mm. (4¼ × 4¼ × $\frac{5}{32}$ in.)	medium glaze	yes
		100 × 100 × 5 mm. (3$\frac{1}{8}$ × 3$\frac{1}{8}$ × $\frac{3}{16}$ in.)	satin and medium glaze	yes
		152 × 152 × 6·5 mm. (6 × 6 × ¼ in.)		
		200 × 100 × 6·5 mm. (7$\frac{7}{8}$ × 3$\frac{1}{8}$ × ¼ in.)		
	Heat-resistant	100 × 100 × 9 mm. (4 × 4 × $\frac{3}{8}$ in.)	satin and medium glaze	some
		152 × 152 × 6·5 mm. (6 × 6 × $\frac{3}{8}$ in.)		
FLOOR TILES	General purpose	100 × 100 × 9·5 mm. (4 × 4 × $\frac{3}{8}$ in.)	unglazed	some
		100 × 100 × 12·5 mm. (4 × 4 × ½ in.)		
		152 × 152 × 12·5 mm. (6 × 6 × ½ in.)		
		200 × 100 × 9·5 mm. (7$\frac{7}{8}$ × 3$\frac{1}{8}$ × $\frac{3}{8}$ in.)		
		200 × 100 × 12·5 mm. (7$\frac{7}{8}$ × 3$\frac{1}{8}$ × ½ in.)		
	Mosaic	610 × 305 mm. (2 × 1 ft) sheets or 305 × 305 mm. (1 × 1 ft) with tiles 25 mm. (1 in.) square or 22 mm. (¾ in.) square	unglazed	no (pre-spaced)

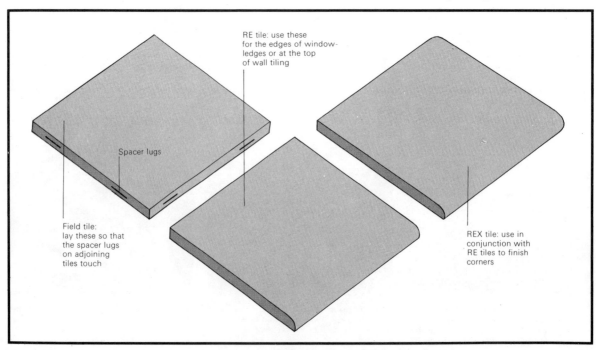

RE tile: use these for the edges of window-ledges or at the top of wall tiling

Spacer lugs

Field tile: lay these so that the spacer lugs on adjoining tiles touch

REX tile: use in conjunction with RE tiles to finish corners

Easy-to-fit bathroom accessories

Most of the major tile manufacturers produce a range of surface-fixing bathroom accessories in colours to match their plain and patterned tiles. These accessories can be applied in the same way as ordinary tiles and are available in the same dimensions (listed on opposite page).

Bath edging

Use ceramic edging cove to seal the gap between the bath and the wall.

The edging is sold in packs which contain sufficient pieces to complete an average-sized bath, as well as four pre-cut mitres for the corners, and two shaped finishing pieces for the ends.

The adhesive is also supplied with the pack—it is rubber based and remains permanently flexible to allow for movement in the bath due to contraction and expansion. The adhesive will stick to glazed tiles, enamel and porcelain, but may have a solvent action on paint, which must be stripped off first.

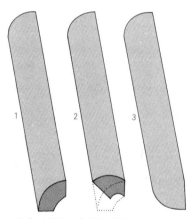

1. Straight trim. 2. Mitred trim for corners.
3. Round end for finishing

Toothbrush rack

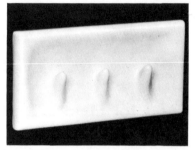

Soap dish

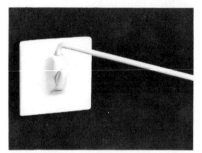

Swivel-arm towel-holder

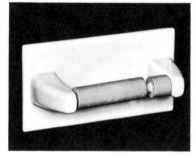

Robe hook

Towel rail ends

Toilet-roll holder

Adhesives and grout

Modern adhesives have almost superseded the old sand and cement method of tile fixing. They are easier to use and give better results. Most can be divided into two groups and classified according to the surfaces for which they are suitable.

Thin bed adhesives: for use on smooth, level surfaces. The adhesive is spread on to the surface and combed out in a layer 1·5–3 mm. ($\frac{1}{16}$–$\frac{1}{8}$ in.) thick. This type of adhesive can be used for all jobs in the home.

Thick bed adhesives: for use on rough and uneven surfaces.

Bal-Flex is suitable for both thick and thin bed application.

In addition, there are adhesives which are intended for specific use in difficult or unusual situations.

Water-resistant adhesives: for tile fixing in areas where there is standing water (shower cubicles etc.).

Heat-resistant adhesives: for use where temperatures are unusually high, for example, the 150°C (302°F) which can be reached around fires and cookers.

Flexible adhesives: for use in areas where some slight degree of background movement may be expected (wooden floors etc.). Listed below are some of the many brands of tile adhesives and their uses.

Grout is a cement-based material for filling the gaps between tiles.

Use water-resistant grout in areas where the tile surface may be exposed to running water, such as around a sink or basin.

Adhesives	Interior/Exterior	Plaster	Old glazed tiles	Building board	Wood	Painted surfaces	Smooth concrete	Cement render	Shower areas	Fireplace surrounds (repairs)
CTF2	Both						√	√	√	√
Bal-Flex	Both	√	√	√	√		√	√	√	√
Bal-Tad	Int	√	√	√	√	√	√	√		
Nic-O-Bond	Both	√	√	√	√	√	√	√		
Cerafix	Both	√	√	√	√	√	√	√		
Polyfix	Both	√	√	√*		√	√	√		
Bal-Proof	Both	√	√	√	√		√	√		
Marley 133	Int	√	√	√	√	√	√			√
Nic-O-Bond W'proof	Both						√	√	√	

*Not on wood composition such as chipboard.

Ceramic tiles/3

Surface preparation

Thorough surface preparation is essential for successful tiling. It must be clean, flat, dry and firm.

Listed below are the main surfaces that you are likely to find and the preparation necessary for each one.

Plaster. A newly plastered surface must be left to dry out for at least one month before tiles are laid on to it. With old plaster, make sure that it is perfectly sound, hacking away and making good any loose areas and removing all loose particles with a dusting brush. Treat porous or dusty plaster with a solvent-based primer such as Bal-Primer, to prevent liquid from the adhesive from being absorbed too quickly.

Paint. If the paint film is sound, tiles can be laid straight on top of it, but if you are in any doubt about the strength of the paint film, then it is best to strip it off. Use a sanding disc, not chemical strippers. Avoid using solvent-based adhesives.

Old ceramic tiles provide a good surface when they are perfectly flat. Repair any chipped or broken tiles with sand and cement or adhesive, and test the remainder to see that they are sticking to the wall properly—any loose tiles must be removed and stuck back on. Wash them down to remove any dirt or grease.

Building boards (plywood, blockboard, chipboard, plasterboard, etc.). These materials provide an ideal surface for tiling, but they must be properly braced so that no movement or warping can take place.

Screw the sheets to 75 × 50 mm. (3 × 2 in.) timbers spaced at 300 mm. (12 in.) centres horizontally and vertically. If the board has a rough and a smooth side, use the former for the working surface as it will provide better adhesion. Seal the back and sides of the board with an ordinary undercoat against moisture penetration.

Brush the surface down thoroughly to remove any dust or loose material, and rub or wash off any grease.

Concrete. Only attempt to lay ceramic tiles on to concrete if the surface is perfectly flat and dry.

Leave new concrete for at least 28 days before laying tiles on to it. Brush dry concrete thoroughly to remove any dust and loose material.

Rough and uneven concrete should be cement screeded before tiles are laid on to it. On slightly uneven concrete use a thick bed adhesive. Rendering a vertical surface such as a wall is a difficult job which is best left to the professional.

Shower areas

Use a water-resistant grade of adhesive for fixing tiles in a shower area.

The surface must be perfectly clean and dry. Apply the adhesive in an even layer about 3 mm. ($\frac{1}{8}$ in.) thick—do not get ridges in it by using a notched trowel.

Allow the tiles to dry for at least 14 days after grouting before using the shower.

Tools for tiling

Notched trowel. Buy a special notched trowel if you intend doing large areas of tiling.

For small areas buy a plastic or metal spreader.

Tile cutter. A scriber with a tungsten carbide tip is the most efficient tool for cutting tiles. A glass cutter can be used, but it will blunt quickly.

Tile nippers. Special tile nippers can be bought, although an ordinary pair of pincers can be used just as efficiently.

Squeegee. This is the easiest tool for grouting, but it is only really essential for floor tiling.

In addition to these tools, you will need: carborundum stone; synthetic sponge; hammer; plumb-line; spirit level; plywood straight-edge.

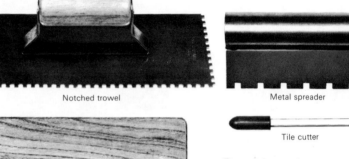
Notched trowel   Metal spreader

Tile cutter

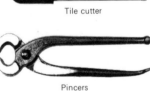
Squeegee   Pincers

Estimating requirements

Tiles. Measure the length and height of the area to be covered. Read off on the adjoining table the number of tiles required for each measurement, and multiply the two numbers to calculate the total required. Add half a dozen to the result to replace breakages.

Use the table to estimate the number of round-edged tiles for each measurement. Order separately from field tiles.

For 152 mm. (6 in.) tiles, measure the length and height of the area in feet to the nearest half-foot, multiply each number by 2, and multiply the two numbers.

To estimate for 100 mm. tiles, take the measurements in millimetres, round the numbers up to the next 100, and multiply the number of hundreds in the two measurements. For 200 mm. tiles, divide this result by 2.

Adhesive. 5 litres (1·1 gallons) of thin bed adhesive covers 5 sq. m. (5$\frac{1}{2}$ sq. yds).

Grout. 1 kg. (2·2 lb.) fills 2 sq. m. (2 sq. yds) of 6 mm. ($\frac{1}{4}$ in.) thick tiles.

mm.	ft in.	No. of tiles	mm.	ft in.	No. of tiles	mm.	ft in.	No. of tiles
108	4$\frac{1}{4}$	1	1620	5 4$\frac{1}{2}$	15	3132	10 5	29
216	8$\frac{1}{2}$	2	1728	5 8$\frac{1}{2}$	16	3240	10 9	30
324	1 0$\frac{1}{2}$	3	1836	6 1	17	3348	11 1$\frac{1}{2}$	31
432	1 5	4	1944	6 5$\frac{1}{2}$	18	3456	11 5$\frac{1}{2}$	32
540	1 9$\frac{1}{2}$	5	2052	6 9$\frac{1}{2}$	19	3564	11 10	33
648	2 1$\frac{1}{2}$	6	2160	7 2	20	3672	12 2$\frac{1}{2}$	34
756	2 6	7	2268	7 6$\frac{1}{2}$	21	3780	12 6$\frac{1}{2}$	35
864	2 10	8	2376	7 10$\frac{1}{2}$	22	3888	12 11	36
972	3 2$\frac{1}{2}$	9	2484	8 3	23	3996	13 3	37
1080	3 7	10	2592	8 7	24	4104	13 7$\frac{1}{2}$	38
1188	3 11	11	2700	8 11$\frac{1}{2}$	25	4212	13 11$\frac{1}{2}$	39
1296	4 3$\frac{1}{2}$	12	2808	9 4	26	4320	14 4	40
1404	4 8	13	2916	9 8	27	4428	14 8	41
1512	5 0	14	3024	10 0$\frac{1}{2}$	28	4536	15 0$\frac{1}{2}$	42

Estimating table. This is for 108 × 108 mm. (4$\frac{1}{4}$ × 4$\frac{1}{4}$ in.) tiles. If one of your wall measurements falls between two dimensions given on the table, use the greater dimension for estimating the number of tiles.

Fixing ceramic wall tiles

Thoroughly clean the surface to be tiled. Find the lowest point on the floor line or skirting and fix a wooden batten to the wall with its upper edge a tile-width above this point [1]. Use a spirit-level to make sure that the batten is perfectly horizontal [2]. The batten can be continued around the room if you are tiling the other walls.

If you intend starting the tiling half-way up the wall, fix the batten on your starting line and make sure that it is horizontal.

Using two tiles with spacer lugs as a guide [3], mark off a number of tile-widths on a spare length of wood and use this as a measuring staff.

With this measuring staff, mark off the batten on the wall [4]. If there is a window work from the centre line below it; if not, work from the centre of the wall. In this way you will avoid narrow cut tiles in the centre of the wall or window.

Plan the tiling so that it is arranged symmetrically around windows and doors, where any narrow cuts will be particularly noticeable.

Decide on which end of the batten you wish to start tiling. Use a spirit level or plumb-line [5] to establish a true vertical at the point where you intend to start, and mark this line on the wall in pencil. Nail a batten along this line to act as your vertical guide.

Check the angle at the intersection of the two battens by placing some tiles loosely in position [6]; they must sit perfectly square.

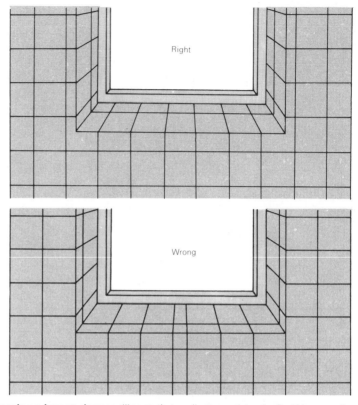

Planning a layout. Arrange tiling so that odd spaces are taken up by cut tiles at the ends of walls (top picture) not in the middle (bottom picture). Position cut tiles on window ledges and recesses at the back (top) not the front (bottom)

1. Fix a horizontal batten with its top a tile-width above the wall's lowest point.

2. Check with a spirit level to get the guide batten perfectly horizontal.

3. Make a measuring staff from a strip of wood marked off in tile-widths.

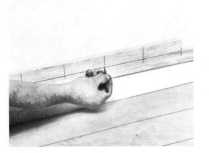

4. Use the measuring staff to mark the batten. Get odd spaces at the ends equal.

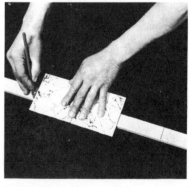

5. Use a level or a plumb-line to get a true vertical for the upright guide batten.

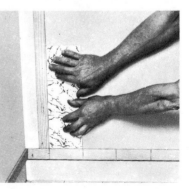

6. Loose tiles should sit perfectly in the angle of the two guide battens. (*continued*)

Tiling walls/2

If your adhesive has to be mixed (most are supplied in a container ready for use), read the instructions on the packet carefully and follow them when mixing.

Use a knife [7] to spread the adhesive over approx. 1 sq. m. (1 sq. yd) of the wall. Use the notched spreader to form ridges in the adhesive [8], pressing it hard against the surface so that the ridges are the same height as the notches on the tool.

In confined spaces where this procedure would be difficult, the adhesive can be buttered on to the backs of the tiles.

Start the tiling at the end of the batten [9] and work in horizontal rows. Press the tiles into the adhesive with a slight twisting action. Tiles must touch the spacer lugs of those next to them or have matchsticks placed between them.

Before spreading another sq. m. of adhesive, check the vertical and horizontal edges of the tiled area with a spirit level [10] to ensure they are accurate. Finish the main area of tiling before returning to fill the odd spaces at the ends of each row.

The top edges of sink units, baths and window-frames are seldom perfectly level, so fix a wooden batten at the height of the nearest line of tiles above the fixture to act as a horizontal guide [11].

Use a pair of pincers and a tile cutter for cutting L-shaped tiles [12] to fit the corners of doors and windows and around light fittings.

Mark and score the tile with a tile cutter [13].

Nibble out the waste in small bites with a pair of pincers [14].

Clean up the edges of the cut with a carborundum stone [15] or file (pincers and a round stone or round file can be used for round or odd-shaped cuts).

7. Apply the adhesive with a stripping knife approx. 1 sq. m. (1 sq. yd) at a time.

8. Ridge the adhesive evenly by drawing the notched spreader hard across it.

9. Start tiling at the intersection of the battens and work in horizontal lines.

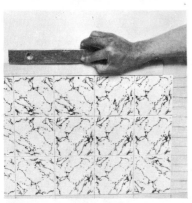

10. Make frequent checks with a spirit level on the horizontal and vertical edges.

11. Fix a guide batten over a top edge for your lowest line of complete tiles.

12. L-shaped tiles can be cut for finishing off at corners of doors and windows.

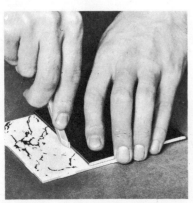

13. Offer the tile to be cut to the wall, mark the waste and score the glazed surface.

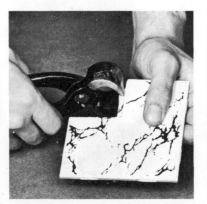

14. Remove the waste from the tile, small pieces at a time, with the pincers.

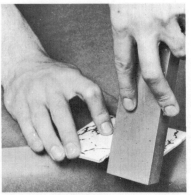

15. Use a carborundum stone to clean and smooth the cut edges of the tile.

When the main area of the tiling is complete, remove the battens.

Level raw edges of cut tiles before fixing them to the wall [16]. Use a carborundum stone, or file if necessary.

When fixing round-edged tiles at external corners, make sure that you allow for the thickness of the tile and the adhesive on the other side of the angle [17].

To measure tiles for the remaining areas, place a tile, back to front [18], over the space it is to fill and mark the cutting edge at two points on the back.

Transfer these marks to the face of the tile and score a line across the glazed surface with the cutter. Place a matchstick under the tile so that it runs back, from the edge, along the line of the cut. Press down gently on the corners of the tile with your thumbs [19]—the tile will break cleanly.

Apply adhesive to the back of the tile [20] and fit the tile with its spacer lugs up against those of adjoining tiles [21].

Tiles to fit along the bottom edge of the wall may have to be trimmed slightly to enable them to fit. Use a pair of pincers and an abrasive stone or file.

Bathroom accessories are fixed in the same way as tiles.

Leave a space in the tiling to take the accessory. Spread adhesive about 1·5 mm. ($\frac{1}{16}$ in.) thick over the back of the accessory and press it in place. Keep it there with tape [22] until the adhesive has set.

Allow the adhesive 24 hours to set before filling the gaps between the tiles with grout. Rub it well in with a sponge [23] and remove the excess with a damp cloth after it has started to dry out. Work over only about 1 sq. m. at a time or the grout may dry before the excess can be cleaned off.

Run a piece of wood with a rounded point along each joint to give it a smooth finish [24]. Allow the grout to dry and then polish the tiles with a soft, dry cloth.

16. Raw edges of cut tiles should be levelled before they are stuck to the wall.

17. At external corners make allowance for the tile edge to be covered.

18. To measure a tile for breaking, offer it to the wall, mark it and score the glaze.

19. A matchstick under the tile and along the scored line will give a clean break.

20. If it is difficult to apply adhesive to the wall, put it on the back of the tile.

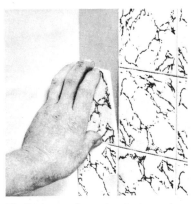

21. Fix the cut tile so that the spacer lugs are against those of adjoining tiles.

22. Hold heavy accessories in place with tape until the adhesive dries.

23. When the tile adhesive has set, use a sponge to fill in the joints with grout.

24. A stick with a rounded point smooths grout between tiles to a uniform finish.

Ceramic tile floors/1

Marking up

Lay ceramic tiles so that they are square in relation to the doorway—when you enter the room the line of tiles must run away squarely from you towards the back of the room. This is particularly important with odd-shaped rooms that are neither square nor rectangular.

Mark a line on the floor [1], at right angles to the doorway, running from the centre of the door to the back of the room.

Take a spare length of wood and divide it into tile lengths (in the same way as described for wall tiling, p. 39). As floor tiles do not have any spacer lugs, you must allow a 3 mm. (⅛ in.) gap between the tiles.

Use this wood as a measuring staff.

Starting from the door jamb with your first full tile, use your measuring staff to divide the centre line off into tile widths [2]. It is very unlikely that a number of full tiles will fit exactly into the length of the room, and you will have to cut tiles to fit right up to the wall. Mark the point near the far wall where the last full tile will finish [2].

Nail a wooden batten [3] across the width of the room at the point where the last full tile finishes. The batten must be at right angles to the centre line, no matter what angle the back wall makes.

Nail another batten at the left-hand end of the first batten to give you a perfectly square corner [4]. This corner is where tiling will start.

The angle between these battens must be accurate since the slightest error at the beginning of the work will be greatly magnified by the time you reach the opposite corner of the room.

You can adjust the position of the second batten if it is important that the cut tiles at either side of the room should be the same size. This is not really important if the tiles are all of the same design and do not have to form a pattern.

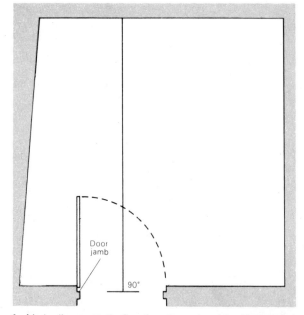

1. Mark a line across the floor from the centre of the doorway and at right angles to it. All work will be based on that line.

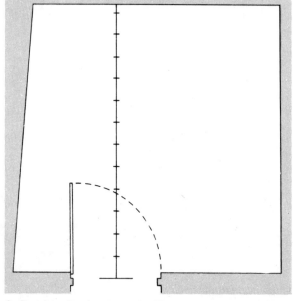

2. Start from the doorway and, with the aid of a measuring staff, mark off the centre line into tile widths.

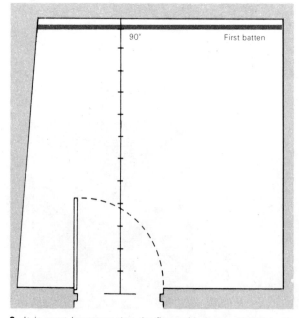

3. It is most important that the first guide batten should be at exactly 90° to the centre line across the floor.

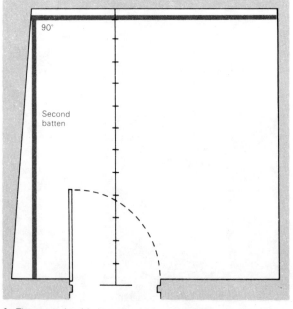

4. The second guide batten must be set at 90° to the first. Check by seeing if it is parallel to the centre line.

Choosing and laying

Ceramic floor tiles are either $100 \times 100 \times 9$ mm. ($4 \times 4 \times \frac{3}{8}$ in.) or $152 \times 152 \times 12$ mm. ($6 \times 6 \times \frac{1}{2}$ in.) and they have a matt, unglazed surface. Unlike wall tiles, most do not have spacer lugs.

Surfaces. Concrete floors are the best surfaces on which to lay ceramic floor tiles. If uneven, they need screeding; if level, an adhesive should be used.

Wood or board-lined floors are suitable surfaces on which to lay ceramic floor tiles.

Make sure that the floor to be tiled is flat and firm—nail down any loose boards and sand the surface if necessary.

Very uneven or rough floors can be lined with resin-bonded ply.

Adhesives. Use an adhesive such as Bal-Flex, which is rubber based and remains permanently flexible to allow for background movement.

Because of the thickness of the floor tiles, some adjustment will have to be made to the doors so that they will fit over the tiles.

Laying procedure: mix the adhesive according to the instructions. Use a plain trowel to spread it over the first square metre (yard) of floor in the corner where you have laid out the battens [1].

Press the tiles into the adhesive [2] and insert spacer pegs in between them [3]. The spaces must be a uniform 3 mm. ($\frac{1}{8}$ in.).

When you have finished the first square metre, scrape off any excess adhesive from around the tiles and coat the next area. Continue in this fashion until the main area of floor is complete.

If your battens were not at the correct angle to start with, you will find that the tiles will gradually get closer together, or further apart, as you work across the room. The only remedy at this stage is to attempt to space the tiles so that they are even. Failing that, you must take them all up and start again with the battens correctly angled at 90°.

When the main area of floor is complete, remove the battens and cut tiles to fit into the spaces round the edges of the room.

Place a tile upside-down over the space to be filled [4] and mark two points to indicate where the tile must be cut (allow 3 mm. for the spacing). Continue these marks around to the face of the tile and score a line across the surface with a tile cutter.

Kneel on the floor and grip a spare tile between your knees. Hold the tile to be cut with one hand on each side of the score line and strike the area of the line on the edge of the tile between your knees [5]. The tile should break cleanly.

Smooth the cut edge with a carborundum stone, rubbing it along, not across, the edge.

Butter the back of the tile with adhesive and place it in position with spacer pegs and with the cut edge up against the wall [6].

Leave the floor for at least 24 hours for the adhesive to set before removing the spacer pegs and rubbing grout into the joints. Grout the floor in the same way as described for wall tiling, but use a rubber squeegee instead of a sponge to make sure that the grout penetrates into the gaps.

After allowing the grout to dry, rub the tiles over with a dry cloth.

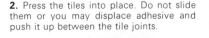

1. Apply adhesive to about 1 sq. m. (1 sq. yd) at a time. This is where a plain trowel comes in handy.

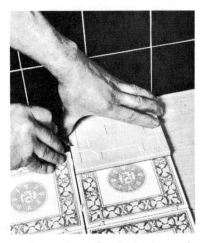

2. Press the tiles into place. Do not slide them or you may displace adhesive and push it up between the tile joints.

3. If you cannot get wooden spacer pegs, use pieces of cardboard with a uniform thickness of about 1·5 mm. ($\frac{1}{16}$ in.).

4. When marking tiles for cutting to fit round the edges of the room, make an allowance of 1·5 mm. for spacer pegs.

5. To get a clean break, use both hands to strike the glazed surface along its scored line against the edge of another tile.

6. The cut edge of the tile should be set against the wall and make a perfect fit after the spacer pegs have been inserted.

Quarry tiling/1

Types and sizes

Quarry tiles are unglazed tiles that provide hard-wearing kitchen, laundry, hall or w.c. floors. They are particularly useful where the floor is liable to become wet.

Quarry tiles can be laid directly on level concrete floors with CTF2 or a thick bed adhesive (see p. 43). On uneven concrete use a cement screed.

Square quarry tiles are made in several sizes from 75 × 75 mm. (3 × 3 in.) to 228 × 228 mm. (9 × 9 in.). The 152 × 152 mm. (6 × 6 in.), usual in domestic work, is made in several thicknesses from 12 to 25 mm. ($\frac{1}{2}$ to 1 in.). The 12 and 15 mm. ($\frac{1}{2}$ and $\frac{5}{8}$ in.) thick tiles are machine made and more tightly compressed than the 22 and 25 mm. ($\frac{7}{8}$ and 1 in.) tiles, which are usually hand made.

Hand-made tiles, like bricks, vary slightly in size, shape and flatness. They have a rougher surface and higher water absorption than the machine-made types.

When a floor with a smooth finish and regular joints is required, 12 or 15 mm. thick machine-made 152 × 152 mm. tiles give best results. Hand-made quarry tiles

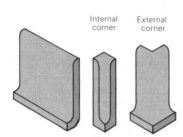

Internal corner External corner

Round-top, cove-base skirting tiles

need wider joints to allow for their irregular shapes.

Red, buff, brown and black are the usual colours of quarry tiles, but others are available in some districts.

Many types of skirting tiles are made for use at the junction of floor and wall. The usual type is rounded on the top edge and coved at the floor junction for easy cleaning. Special tiles are made for use on internal and external angles and at stopped ends.

Round-edge RE and REX tiles (see p. 36) are made for edging steps and sills.

Cutting quarry tiles

Rectangular tiles, 152 mm. (6 in.) long, are made in several widths, but sometimes tiles have to be cut to finish a floor.

Cut the tile about 3 mm. ($\frac{1}{8}$ in.) smaller than the gap, to allow for the joint. Chalk the line first; then score the tile deeply with a tile cutter, along a metal straight-edge.

Set the tile on the floor and place a short metal bar under it, in line with the cut. Press the tile against the floor and strike the other side.

Make curved cuts by breaking the tile to the nearest straight line, then nibbling away the rest with pincers.

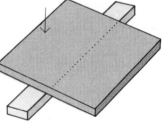

Pressure snaps the tile along the scored line

Laying tiles on a concrete floor

Calculate the number of tiles needed and plan the layout so that you do not finish with very narrow tiles along any wall.

If you are using hand-made tiles, soak them in water for several hours before you begin work. Clean any cement droppings, grease or oil off the concrete floor.

Cut two gauge rods from planed timber. Make them the same length as a row of six tiles with 3 mm. ($\frac{1}{8}$ in.) joints between them. Mark the joint positions on the rods.

Lay the gauge rods out from the straight wall at 90° and lay a batten against their ends, parallel to the wall. Nail it to the floor, remove the gauge rods and place a second batten against the wall. Use battens that are twice as thick as the tiles.

Use a spirit level to check that the battens are level [1]. Use small pieces of wood as packing to level the battens, prising up

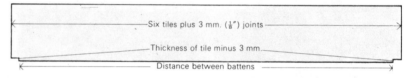

Six tiles plus 3 mm. ($\frac{1}{8}$") joints

Thickness of tile minus 3 mm.

Distance between battens

Dimensions of combined dragging board and straight-edge

the nailed batten slightly where necessary.

Next cut a dragging board, the same length as the gauge rods, from a wide piece of timber with straight, parallel edges. At each corner on one edge, cut a notch 3 mm. ($\frac{1}{8}$ in.) shallower than the tiles' thickness, so that the board fits between the battens.

For the bedding, use a 1 : 3 cement-sand mix. Building sand is suitable. The mix should be neither so dry as to be crumbly nor so wet as to allow the tiles to sink.

Spread the mix between the battens with a steel float [2]. Then drag it, with the dragging board between the battens, until you have a smooth, level finish over slightly more than the first area to be tiled [3].

Lift the batten from the wall and fill the gap with bedding, using a trowel [4]. Dust the bedding with dry cement, to provide a strong key for the tiles.

Lay a row of tiles between the wall and the other batten, using a gauge rod.

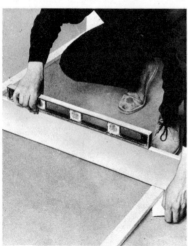

1. Set out the battens and check they are level. Pack low spots with pieces of wood.

2. Spread the bedding mix over the area of the first tiles with a steel float.

3. Drag the board between the battens to get a smooth, level surface on the bedding.

4. Fill the gap left by the wall batten with mix, maintaining the level surface.

5. Lay a row of tiles and lay the dragging board parallel to them, using the gauge rods.

6. Beat the tiles down with a wooden block until they are level with the batten.

7. Run the trowel along the joints to straighten the tiles after beating them down.

8. Rub the grout into the joints with a rubber squeegee. Remove excess grout.

9. Wash over with a soapless detergent when the grout is thoroughly dry.

Set out the gauge rods from this first row of tiles and place the uncut edge of the dragging board against their ends [5].

Lift the gauge rods and lay rows of tiles along the batten—again using the gauge rod to space them—then along the dragging board and the wall until all the edges of the area are covered. Then fill the centre.

If, at this stage, the bedding has hardened so that the tiles do not move when touched, brush water into the joints.

Next, beat the tiles down to the level of the battens, tapping them with the face of a block of 100 × 50 mm. timber [6].

Straighten the tiles by running the trowel along the joints [7]. Wash the tiles clean with a sponge and water.

Replacing broken tiles

Remove a broken quarry tile from the floor by breaking it up with a hammer and small cold chisel, starting at its centre to avoid damage to adjacent tiles. If adjacent tiles are not firmly bedded, lift them out.

Set the wall batten in place again and lay the next area of bedding between the battens, first dusting the edge of the first area with dry cement.

When one strip is tiled, remove the fixed batten and set out the battens for the second strip, working from the edge of the first strip. Dust the edge of the bedding with dry cement before laying each area of the second strip.

When the whole floor is tiled, strip by strip, leave the bedding to harden for 24 hours before grouting the tiles.

When you have to stand on the floor while grouting, cover the tiles with a large piece of chipboard—about 900 × 600 mm. (3 × 2 ft)—to prevent them moving.

Chisel any projections off the bedding and set the new tiles in position—dry, to check that they do not project above floor level. New tiles must be identical in size and thickness to existing tiles.

Use a pure cement mix for grouting. Rub the grout between the tiles with a squeegee [8].

Remove as much surplus grout as possible with the squeegee. Then rub a softwood stick with a rounded end along the joints.

Work over the tiles with a pad of cloth to clean them and absorb any bits of cement. Rub diagonally across the joints at first, then along them.

Wash down the tiles with a soapless detergent [9] and give them a final rub-over with a clean cloth.

If the tiles are outdoors do not polish them. Finish indoor tiles with proprietary tile polish.

If only two or three tiles are to be replaced, bed the new ones with Bal-Tad or similar adhesive. If many tiles are to be re-laid, hack up the bedding and re-lay as for a new floor.

Mosaic floor tiles

Laying paper-backed sheets

Mosaic tiles are sold in paper-backed sheets, either 610 × 305 mm. (2 × 1 ft) or 305 × 305 mm. (1 × 1 ft). The tiles are either square or rectangular.

Laying hexagonal mosaics is best left to a professional. The details of surfaces and adhesives are the same as for the 152 × 152 mm. floor tiles (see pp. 42–43).
Laying procedure: mark up and batten the floor in the same way as described for floor tiles, and apply adhesive to the floor (see previous pages).

Apply grout to the back of a sheet of mosaic with a trowel [1] (the face of the mosaic is the side with the paper on it). Use a rubber squeegee to press the grout well into the gaps between the individual tiles [2]. Do not allow the sheet to soak for too long before laying it, otherwise the water in the grout will loosen the paper backing before you are ready. Ensure that the back of the sheet is free of grout before laying.

Place the sheet of mosaic in position on the floor and space other sheets around it at the same distance apart as are the individual mosaics [3].

Use a home-made wooden tool to tamp the sheets of mosaic down hard so that all the individual tiles are evenly bedded into the adhesive [4]. Remove any excess adhesive from around the tiles before going on to the next square yard.

When you have finished the main area of the floor, remove the battens and cut tiles to fit the gaps around the edges [5]. If you are fortunate, complete mosaics will fill the gaps. If they do not, you will have to score the individual tiles and break them with a pair of pincers. Spread adhesive on to the floor and tamp the tiles down [6] in the same way as described above.

Allow the paper to soak for a while [7], then peel it gently off the tiles [8].

Apply more grout with a squeegee [9] to fill the gaps where the sheets met.

1. Apply grout to the back of the mosaic sheet (this is the side without paper on it).

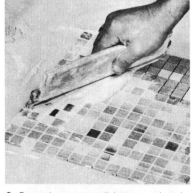

2. Press the grout well home so that the gaps between the tiles are filled.

3. The distance between the sheets should be the same as between the tiles.

4. Tamp the sheets down so that they are properly bedded into the adhesive.

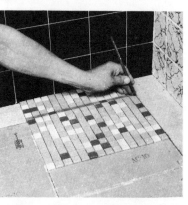

5. Mark the edge to be cut after laying the sheet, upside-down, over the vacant area.

6. Grout the cut sheet before setting it in place and bedding it down.

7. When the adhesive is set, soak the papered surfaces with water.

8. Peel the paper off to expose the face of the mosaic tiles.

9. Fill the gaps where the sheets met with grout. Clean off any surplus.

Metrication tables

USE THESE scales to convert feet and inches into centimetres or millimetres. Convert from feet to metres with the scale on the far right of the page. Convert inches into centimetres or millimetres by comparing the exact measurement on the inch scale with the corresponding measurement on the metric scale. For example, 1 in. equals 2·54 cm. or 25·4 mm. Similarly, 1 ft 1½ in. equals 34·3 cm. (343 mm.).

Convert centimetres or millimetres into inches by comparing the measurement on the metric scale with the corresponding unit on the inch scale. For example, 64 cm. equals 2 ft $1\frac{3}{16}$ in., and 11mm equals $\frac{7}{16}$ in.

inches	mm.	inches	mm.	inches	mm.	inches	mm.	feet	metres
sixteenths	1cm.	10in.	26cm.	1ft 8in.	51cm.	2ft 6in.	76cm.		
	2cm.		27cm.		52cm.		77cm.	1ft	30·5cm.
1 in.	3cm.	11in.	28cm.	1ft 9in.	53cm.	2ft 7in.	78cm.		
	4cm.		29cm.		54cm.		79cm.		
2 in.	5cm.	12in.	30cm.		55cm.		80cm.	2ft	61·0cm.
	6cm.		31cm.	1ft 10in.	56cm.	2ft 8in.	81cm.		
	7cm.		32cm.		57cm.		82cm.	3ft	91·4cm.
3 in.	8cm.	1ft 1in.	33cm.	1ft 11in.	58cm.		83cm.	3ft 3⅜in.	1 metre
	9cm.		34cm.		59cm.	2ft 9in.	84cm.		(100cm.)
4 in.	10cm.		35cm.		60cm.		85cm.	4ft	121·9cm.
	11cm.	1ft 2in.	36cm.	2ft	61cm.		86cm.		
	12cm.		37cm.		62cm.	2ft 10in.	87cm.		
5 in.	13cm.	1ft 3in.	38cm.		63cm.		88cm.	5ft	152·4cm.
	14cm.		39cm.	2ft 1in.	64cm.		89cm.		
6 in.	15cm.		40cm.		65cm.	2ft 11in.	90cm.	6ft	182·9cm.
	16cm.	1ft 4in.	41cm.	2ft 2in.	66cm.		91cm.		
	17cm.		42cm.		67cm.	3ft	92cm.	6ft 6¾in.	2 metres
7 in.	18cm.	1ft 5in.	43cm.		68cm.		93cm.	7ft	213·4cm.
	19cm.		44cm.	2ft 3in.	69cm.		94cm.		
	20cm.		45cm.		70cm.	3ft 1in.	95cm.		
8 in.	21cm.	1ft 6in.	46cm.	2ft 4in.	71cm.		96cm.	8ft	243·8cm.
	22cm.		47cm.		72cm.	3ft 2in.	97cm.		
9 in.	23cm.	1ft 7in.	48cm.	2ft 5in.	73cm.		98cm.	9ft	274·3cm.
	24cm.		49cm.		74cm.	3ft 3in.	99cm.		
	25cm.		50cm.		75cm.		100cm.	9ft 10⅛in.	3 metres (300cm.)

Page 47

Other titles in this series:

THE USE AND CARE OF LAWN MOWERS
LOOKING AFTER YOUR CAR (In Preparation)

In case of difficulty, order direct from
The Reader's Digest Circulation Department,
25 Berkeley Square, London W1X 6AB

Published by The Reader's Digest Association
Limited, 25 Berkeley Square, London W1X 6AB

First edition
Copyright © 1975 The Reader's Digest
Association Limited

Printed in Great Britain by Varnicoat Limited,
Pershore, Worcestershire